SUPERSTAR GUITARS

TONE SWITCH
1
2
3

SUPERSTAR GUITARS

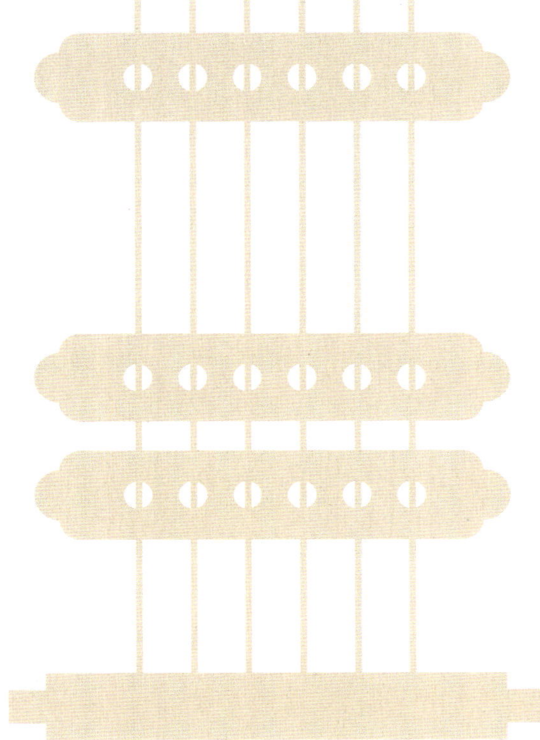

EXPLORE THE GUITARS THAT CHANGED MUSIC FOREVER

ELEANOR JANE

CONTENTS

FOREWORD

In 1991, Nicky Wire, Sean Moore and Richey James Edwards suggested I buy a white Les Paul Custom with our first record company advance, an act of generosity I have never really expressed enough gratitude for. That guitar has offered me inspiration, confidence, solutions and a sense of being able to channel something. As a utilitarian tool, an object of beauty, whatever it may be, it is beyond precious to me.

Who knew that Guthrie's Martin acoustic could kill fascists? Who would have guessed Dylan's Fender Stratocaster could incite accusations of betrayal and apostasy. I have been to concerts where a guitarist I admired failed to use their trademark guitar and the experience was somehow hollow. That guitar is part of them in my mind, their history and very identity; why have they forsaken it?

All a bit dramatic, I know, but that's how this book makes you feel about these guitars. The photos show their beauty, but also their damage and the scars of time that bind them to their players. When Eleanor photographed my guitar "Faithful", she insisted on showing its age and experience by focusing on some of its imperfections and time-worn deterioration.

Hendrix's Woodstock Stratocaster seems like an untouchable emperor, Jack White's Valco Airline looks like a new type of superhero, Thurston Moore's Jazzmaster is simply hypnotising. The photographs feel personal and Eleanor captures them with clarity and warmth. I've fallen in love with so many of these guitars, I hope you do too.

James Dean Bradfield

ET 2
NORMAL
Fender

INTRODUCTION

Throughout the pages of this book you'll see iconic guitars in intimate detail, the way I have been fortunate enough to see them; up close and personal, photographed backstage at concert venues, festivals, museums, recording studios and even in artists' private homes.

It's a strange area in which to specialize, but for the past decade and a half I have photographed some of music's most culturally significant and valuable guitars, as well as the people that play them.

My journey began with a commission to photograph Rory Gallagher's famously beaten-up Stratocaster for a pull-out poster in *Guitar World* magazine. The guitar work kept coming and before long I was travelling the world, photographing extravagant vintage collections, legendary guitars that had been in the hands of the greats and all sorts of curios in between.

I fell in love with the work and was astounded at the doors guitars could open. Artists would invite me into their creative spaces and candidly share stories about their most beloved instruments. Chatting with Dave Grohl in the Foo Fighters' private rehearsal room or pausing mid photoshoot so Jack White could make a voice note of a guitar riff he'd just come up with are two favourite recent memories.

I've always tried to treat the guitars I shoot as beautiful objects and historic pieces, but not in a staid, clinical way. I light them to bring out the warmth of the flame, the hairline cracks of checked lacquer and the play-wear that reveals something about the artist's connection with the instrument. The sixpence dust between the pickups on Brian May's Red Special, for example, or the way in which the sunburst paintwork is worn right down to the woodgrain on John Frusciante's 1962 Fender Stratocaster.

One of the most enjoyable parts of this project has been writing the chapters on blues legends Bukka White and Howlin' Wolf. Although I knew and loved their music already, my encounters with it had always been fragmentary – a song here or there, perhaps discovered after hearing a cover version and tracing it back to the original source. I knew very little about their personal lives. But the stories! Separating fact from rich, colourful folklore has been almost impossible. Back then, people lived much more itinerant lives that could be chaotic, difficult, often violent. But in order to be somebody you had to be somewhere; travelling to record, to perform, to be a part of the scene. Their guitars were with them on every step of those journeys, and the cracks, chips and scratches that adorn them offer us a window back to that time.

When these guitars and their stories are collected, similar themes emerge. On either side of the pond in the 1990s, two guitars that appear in this book were used to create music that caused a genuine cultural shift, inspiring millions to pick up the guitar for the first time: Noel Gallagher's Epiphone Riviera from the *(What's The Story) Morning Glory?* era and the Fender Mustang played by Kurt Cobain in the music video for "Smells Like Teen Spirit".

On the road, touring artists would often stop off at independent music stores and it's these places that defined the guitar-buying experience. So many legendary guitar acquisition stories feature the romance of a serendipitous discovery in a mom and pop store somewhere left of nowhere. Some of these locations became legendary haunts for musicians in their own right, such as Manny's Music in New York City. Although it is sadly long gone, artists from all over the world – and several in this book – discovered their number-one guitars inside those brownstone walls.

Another recurring theme is that of the guitar as an object of protest; using the instrument as both a literal and figurative canvas for spreading a political message. Almost half a century apart, Woody Guthrie and Tom Morello scrawled or scraped messages of protest into the wood of their guitars. Even today, the guitar still has currency as a countercultural object. Phoebe Bridgers' act of guitar smashing at the end of an *SNL* performance sparked a backlash, yet the fragments of numerous instruments smashed by male performers that came before her are displayed in museums. In the right hands, even the old rock 'n' roll tropes still have the power to shock.

The final guitar I photographed especially for this book brought me full circle. James Dean Bradfield's 1990 Gibson Les Paul Custom provided the soundtrack to my early years as a photography student, riding the bus to college listening to cassette tapes of local superstars, Manic Street Preachers. In those days, although I dabbled with a bit of guitar playing myself, I certainly didn't imagine that guitars would feature as prominently as they have in my future career. It's been a fantastic journey so far – I hope you enjoy this collection.

Eleanor Jane

VOX
'59 GIBSON

NATIONAL
DUOLIAN

BUKKA WHITE

Hard Rock – 1933 National Duolian

What a story this beautifully worn National Duolian resonator could tell of a life scuffed and slid through the Delta by trailblazing Mississippi bluesman, Booker "Bukka" T. Washington White. First cousin of B.B. King and one-time resident of the Mississippi State Penitentiary, White played this guitar well into the latter years of his career until it almost wore out. One of his setlists is still taped to the side of the body – a handwritten scrawl on notepaper courtesy of the Hotel Leamington, the tape brittle and yellowed but holding strong even now.

Born on a Mississippi farm sometime between 1900 and 1909 (it's not clear if he knew the exact date himself), White began his musical journey playing the fiddle at local square dances before receiving his first guitar as a ninth-birthday gift from his father. Married at around 16 years old, only to lose his young wife a few years later due to a burst appendix, what followed was a life on and off the road, working blue-collar jobs when necessary and travelling the emerging blues scene between Memphis and Chicago.

The musical world that the young Bukka White inhabited in the 1930s was still very much a time when songs were passed between musicians in the oral tradition. While not exactly simpler times by any means for a Southern Black man in the Great Depression, there is a purity in the idea of the itinerant musician travelling America with just one guitar and a songbook in their head full of raw, biographical stories – both original and inherited – that express the real-life experiences of everyday people.

While it's hard to validate some of Bukka's tales – he seems to have held true to the old adage "never let the truth get in the way of a good story" – he certainly ran into plenty of trouble along the road. In 1937, White made his first Chicago recordings ("Pinebluff Arkansas" and "Shake 'Em On Down") but by the time they were released he was in prison, serving time for murder after being convicted of shooting a man in the thigh.

Christened "Hard Rock" by White, his 1933 Duolian was deemed a "holy relic" by B.B. King. Like many technological innovations in the world of guitar, resonators were designed to generate volume – an analogue amplifier in a world before electrification. In White's hands, played with a slide in open tunings and even beaten like a drum, Hard Rock lived up to its name, underpinning his voice with raucous accompaniment.

NATIONAL
DUOLIAN

Bigsby

HOWLIN' WOLF

1965 Epiphone Casino

Of all the trailblazing electric blues singers, Howlin' Wolf not only had the biggest physical presence – reported variously as anything from 6ft 3in to 6ft 7in in height and never far short of 300lb – he also had arguably the greatest and certainly the most unique voice, seemingly clearing the demons from his throat. Record producer Sam Phillips, best known for first putting Elvis Presley in the studio and someone who knew a thing or two about raw talent, described Wolf's voice as "the sound of a man's soul".

Born Chester Arthur Burnett in White Station, Mississippi in 1910, Wolf was the youngest of six children and had a difficult childhood, growing up in poverty in the rural South. He was nicknamed "Wolf" by his grandfather, who told him the big, bad wolf would take him away if he misbehaved. While he was still a young boy, Wolf's mother threw him out of the family home, forcing him to walk barefoot across frozen fields to the home of an abusive great uncle, a man he described as "the meanest man between here and hell".

If that sounds like character-building stuff, he would later inhabit the physiology of the wolf as an artist, stalking back and forth across the stage and even crawling across the boards on all fours. The Wolf's famous howl, meanwhile, was the result of attempting to emulate country star Jimmie Rodgers' yodel.

In the 1930s, Wolf crossed paths with a laundry list of Delta blues originators, learning blues guitar and showmanship from Charley Patton and sharing stages with Robert Johnson and Son House. In 1941, Wolf was enlisted in the US Army and assigned to the 9th Cavalry Regiment, one of the units known as "Buffalo Soldiers".

He worked in the kitchen, where he would cook meals for his fellow soldiers during the day and play guitar for them at night in the mess hall. It was at one of these informal evening performances at Fort Gordon, Georgia, that a young James Brown apparently first heard him play while visiting the fort to earn extra money shining the soldiers' shoes and dancing.

Although he learned to play guitar as a teenager, once he began working with a band, Wolf left most of the guitar playing to his longtime right-hand man Hubert Sumlin. However, Wolf still played frequently and one of his most recognizable guitars is this 1965 Epiphone Casino, most famously seen in a photoshoot that later graced the covers of several albums and now part of the collection at the Museum of Pop Culture (MoPOP) in Seattle. This is also the guitar he played on his European tour. On one memorable night, he prowled the stage of the Romford Odeon with a towel tucked into his waistband to create a tail, climbed ten feet up the theatre's stage curtains and then slid all the way back down, all the while blowing on a harmonica, no doubt terrifying the audience. Had the big, bad wolf come to take them away?

Bigsby
PATENT
D-169,120

VOLUME
VOLUME
TONE
TONE

Epiphone

TONE

WOODY GUTHRIE

1936 Martin 000-18

Bob Dylan's poem "Last Thoughts On Woody Guthrie" was recited live only once, at New York City's Town Hall. After performing several new songs at the concert on 12 April 1963, Dylan returned to the stage to recite the poem. He explained that he had been asked to write a piece for the introduction of an upcoming book about Woody Guthrie: "What does Woody Guthrie mean to you, in twenty-five words? I couldn't do it. I wrote out five pages. I have it here by accident, actually. And I'd like to say this out loud."

What followed was a seven-minute poem that travels through all our small daily heartaches and troubles, eventually painting Woody Guthrie as an emblem of hope in a mixed-up world. Delivered to an audience in pin-drop silence until they erupted in rapturous applause at the end, the reading takes on extreme poignancy when you consider that Guthrie, hospitalized by Huntington's disease, would soon be unable to speak and would pass away at the age of 55, in 1967. Dylan idolized him and was a regular visitor. Describing Guthrie's work in volume one of his memoir, *Chronicles*, Dylan wrote: "The songs themselves, his repertoire, were really beyond category. They had the infinite sweep of humanity in them... Woody Guthrie tore everything in his path to pieces. To me [his music] was an epiphany."

Woody Guthrie was born in 1912 into a middle-class family in Oklahoma. He had a natural talent for music, teaching himself to play guitar, harmonica, banjo and violin to a competent standard. He preferred to keep his musical compositions simple and relatable so they wouldn't sound too polished and off-putting for common folk. During the Dust Bowl era, Guthrie joined the thousands of other Okies who made the trip west to California in search of jobs. A champion of inclusivity and social justice, and a supporter of migrant workers, he sought to empower the working man through his music.

It is believed that he used this Martin 000-18 in the late 1930s, during his time in Los Angeles. "Woody" is carved into the back, along with "This Machine Kills Fascists". It's thought to be the earliest appearance of the slogan on one of his guitars – by the early 1940s it would be painted or affixed to the front of several of his other instruments, but their fate is unknown, and only this Martin survives from Guthrie's most politically-charged era.

While the chronology is blurry, the sentiment endures – music, culture and creativity are the best weapons we have to fight against oppression. Although violent, it is ultimately a message of hope that through unity we will find freedom.

Woody

this machine kills fascists

Fender
TONE
TONE

BOB DYLAN

Newport Folk Festival – 1964 Fender Stratocaster

One of the most culturally significant guitars in rock folklore (or should that be folk-rock lore?!) is the 1964 Fender Stratocaster with which Bob Dylan first "went electric" in public at the Newport Folk Festival in July 1965. Much myth and legend surrounds that event – the crowd, accustomed to hearing Dylan playing solo with little more than an acoustic guitar and a Hohner Marine Band harmonica, booed with gusto at the new direction. As Dylan and his band worked their way through a short set of "Maggie's Farm", "Like A Rolling Stone" and "Phantom Engineer", the organizer threatened to cut the power cord to the stage with an axe, and Dylan was declared a traitor to the folk cause. Or so the stories go.

But the Stratocaster itself was just a forgettable tool in the whole circus of the event. It was discarded by Dylan on the airplane journey back from Rhode Island, taken home by the pilot and stored in a closet for decades. The guitar wasn't played again for many years, remaining just as Dylan left it. Even today it's like something from a time capsule, plucked from that historic moment in pop culture and brought into the now. Indeed, visually it still has the vibe of a brand-new Strat fresh from Fender's original factory in Fullerton, California.

Perhaps fittingly, in person the guitar doesn't give anything away – it's just as enigmatic and mysterious as Dylan himself. It's a strange guitar to encounter; a classic 1964 three-tone Sunburst Strat – desirable, yet at the same time very ordinary. The nitrocellulose finish is vibrant and unfaded; glossy and clean with no telltale wear patterns to suggest anything about the artist's playing style, and no modifications that betray his sonic preferences. If this guitar has secrets, it's concealing them very well indeed.

How very Bob Dylan, to strap on a guitar, change the course of history and then cast it aside.

Fender
STRATOCASTER
WITH SYNCHRONIZED TREMOLO
ORIGINAL
Contour Body

VOLUME
TONE
TONE

VOLUME
TONE
TONE

Fender Tremolux
FULLERTON, CALIFORNIA

DAVE DAVIES

The Kinks

1958 Gibson Flying V

By 1965 the British invasion was in full flow and American teenagers were rocking to the sound of energetic young beat groups from across the Atlantic. With the lyrical and melodic intelligence of frontman Ray Davies and the brute force of his brother Dave's riffs, The Kinks fused the pop savvy of The Beatles with the danger of The Rolling Stones and The Who. They could have had it all... until hard drinking and a dispute with a promoter over payment resulted in The Kinks being banned from touring America for four years.

At some point during that chaotic 1965 tour, Dave Davies' Guild Starfire was lost by an airline. Needing a replacement, fast, he wandered into a guitar shop and picked out a strangely shaped guitar on the back wall. The image of Dave Davies playing his Gibson Flying V on the TV show *Shindig!* is now iconic, but it was a bumpy ride for the futuristic electric guitar design that Gibson introduced alongside the similarly angular Explorer in 1958.

In the mid to late 1950s, Gibson sought to invigorate their sales with a line of more modernistic solidbody guitars, in competition with Fender's sleek new Stratocaster, which was already a big hit. The Flying V was made from lightweight African limba wood (named korina by Gibson) with gold-plated hardware. But even though it was the atomic age, the guitar-playing public weren't quite ready for this version of the future and the guitars didn't sell well at all. Only 98 Flying Vs were manufactured between 1958 and 1959 before the model was discontinued. A handful were later assembled from leftover bodies and necks in 1963. As a result of this scarcity and the impact of players such as Dave Davies, Albert King and Lonnie Mack, original korina Flying Vs are among the most sought-after vintage instruments on the planet.

Today you are more likely to see a Flying V in the hands of a heavy metal guitarist, which seems fitting when you consider that Dave Davies was one of the pioneers of the heavily distorted powerchord, a significant influence on the punk and metal scenes that followed.

After coming up for sale at auction in 2019, the guitar now resides with a friend of mine in Palm Springs, collector and musician Gary Gand. Though it has a repair to the heel, it still has the PAF pickups that were fitted at the factory. Some of the tuning pegs have crumbled and been replaced, but those that remain are a fantastic example of the deterioration into mummy's teeth that often befalls these early, unstable vintage plastics. Happily, Gary occasionally gigs the guitar around Palm Springs, and I can think of no better location to hear a true icon of mid-century guitar design in person.

Gibson

VOX

GEORGE HARRISON

The Beatles

1964 Gibson SG Standard

George Harrison was still only 23 years old in April 1966, when The Beatles went into EMI Studios to record what would become their seventh studio album in three years and perhaps their greatest work, *Revolver.*

Unlike many modern guitar heroes, George owned and used a relatively small number of instruments during The Beatles' seven-year recording career. He acquired this 1964 Gibson SG Standard in 1966 and played it extensively during the *Revolver* sessions. This was his first Gibson solidbody and a favourite instrument between 1966 and 1968.

Following the twang and jangle of the Gretsch and Rickenbacker models that characterized their early beat-group sound, a significant gear shift came during the *Revolver* era when The Beatles simultaneously developed both a woozy psychedelic edge and embraced more abrasive rock-guitar textures.

It was a sign of the times; everything was beginning to sound a bit tougher. The Rolling Stones and The Yardbirds were championing the American blues artists from which so much music drew its inspiration, and technology was changing. Fuzz pedals had arrived on the scene, guitar amplifiers were easier to distort, and a wider palette of sounds and textures was available to artists. The Beatles were early adopters, who loved playing around with new gear and pushing the limits of recording techniques, with the unsettling sound of reverse tape effects being one of their most memorable creative experiments.

Other than the promotional videos for "Paperback Writer" and "Rain", the most extensive footage of George's SG was captured during the recording of "Hey

Bulldog" in EMI's Studio Three in February 1968. As well as being employed by George for the song's menacing riff, John Lennon can be seen noodling away on the SG on film, and he is thought to have borrowed George's guitar to record the song's guitar solo.

Although George was clearly a convert to Gibson solidbodies with humbuckers at this point, by the following year he had passed the SG on to one of the artists on The Beatles' label, Apple Records – Pete Ham of Badfinger. After being used on a string of Badfinger hits, the guitar later came into the possession of Pete Ham's brother, John, who sold it to the Jim Irsay Collection.

Gibson

Gibson

VOX
GRETSCH
BY
Bigsby

JOHN LENNON

The Beatles

1963 Gretsch 6120 Chet Atkins

This double-cutaway 1963 Gretsch 6120 Chet Atkins model was known to be one of the instruments that John Lennon kept in his private music room in the converted loft space of his sprawling Tudor-style home in Weybridge, Surrey.

Before The Beatles went into the studio to record their seventh studio album, *Revolver*, Paul McCartney visited John at home for a songwriting session, developing the idea that became the lyrics to "Paperback Writer" in the car on the journey over. Although their songwriting process evolved over the years, at this stage it was very relaxed and, like most British people, their working day began with a cup of tea.

"You knew, the minute you got there, cup of tea and you'd sit and write," McCartney recalled in conversation with author Barry Miles for the 1997 biography, *Paul McCartney: Many Years From Now*. "It was always good if you had a theme... I arrived at Weybridge and told John I had this idea of trying to write to a publisher to become a paperback writer, and I said, 'I think it should be written like a letter.'"

The song would develop into an unconventional classic – innovative both in narrative form and arrangement, thanks to the a cappella intro featuring John, Paul and George's vocals. It's something unexpected in the context of a pop single, but instinctive and natural to friends who had sung together since their teens, practising harmonies in the enclosed porch of John's Aunt Mimi's house in Liverpool. Today, that home is owned by the National Trust and it is possible to tour the building and hear your own voice reverberating off the original tiles.

"Paperback Writer" was recorded over two days in April 1966, during the sessions for *Revolver* at EMI Studios. On day two – 14 April – a photographer from *Beatles Monthly*, Leslie Bryce, was in the studio to capture John using his 6120 in a series of images, which many years later would be used to authenticate the instrument.

John had an even tighter roster of instruments than George, and several of his guitars remain with his family. In November 1967, John gifted the Gretsch to his younger cousin, David Birch, who was trying to get a band together at the time. Birch, visiting his cousin in Weybridge, apparently had his eye on another guitar in the music room, John's Sonic Blue Fender Stratocaster, but Lennon suggested he take the Gretsch instead. Birch used it for years before it was sold at auction in 2015 to guitar collector Jim Irsay.

GRETSCH

U.S. PAT.
2892371

VOX
GRETSCH
BY
Bigsby

VOLUME
TONE
TONE

JIMI HENDRIX

Woodstock Strat – 1968 Fender Stratocaster

Could Jimi Hendrix's 1968 Olympic White Fender Stratocaster be the most iconic guitar of all time? Owned by the most iconic guitarist, who used it to play the most iconic piece of American music while closing out the most iconic festival in rock history, there's certainly a strong case for it.

The legendary Woodstock Festival of 1969 had been plagued by technical issues and scheduling delays. Having been due to perform at midnight, Hendrix and his new band Gypsy Sun and Rainbows finally took to the stage at 9am on Monday 18 August. Not exactly a traditional slot for a festival headliner, but I suppose with so many drugs floating around, circadian rhythms were pretty out of whack.

Although the festival attendance peaked at around 400,000, some 30,000 people stuck it out until the Monday morning and witnessed Hendrix's set, which culminated in a distorted and improvisational solo performance of "The Star-Spangled Banner" – a protest against the Vietnam War that signalled both the end of the Sixties and the death of the Summer of Love.

Jimi's guitar was purchased in 1968 at Manny's Music in New York City and, aside from a few minor customizations made to accommodate his left-handedness, it remained stock. A relatively mundane tool, perhaps, but Hendrix could conjure incredible soundscapes from very little with an astonishing level of creativity.

Instruments that have genuinely been used and played by Jimi Hendrix are extremely valuable and incredibly difficult to track down, with many reduced to mere shards of splintered wood. Miraculously, the Woodstock guitar has remained intact.

Today, residing at MoPOP in Seattle, the guitar is in remarkably clean condition, although much of that seems to be down to enthusiastic cleaning when it first came up for sale in the 1990s. The slightest hint of a cigarette burn is still visible on the headstock, along with some scuffs and dents in the body, but a sense of magic is still there.

No doubt Hendrix could have made a psychedelic masterpiece out of an elastic band on a stick, but there's something very special about being able to encounter such an important piece of music and cultural history.

VOLUME
1 2 3 5 6
TONE
10 1 2

VOLUME

Fender
STRATOCASTER
VOLUME
TONE
TONE

J.GARCIA

JERRY GARCIA

Grateful Dead

Tiger – Doug Irwin

There is no such thing as a casual Grateful Dead fan. Formed in 1965 in the San Francisco Bay Area – where else? – few bands have ever been as eclectic, and it's hard to think of a more loyal and devoted fanbase than the legion of Deadheads; a whole subculture brought together by the unifying power of music, along with a little herbal accompaniment.

Grateful Dead frontman Jerry Garcia was clearly not a guitarist who was easily satisfied by off-the-peg instruments. Almost immediately after receiving Wolf, a previous custom-build from luthier Doug Irwin, Garcia commissioned Tiger, telling Irwin to create the most extravagant guitar he was capable of. It was a dream assignment for any luthier and Irwin certainly fulfilled the brief.

The project would take 2,000 hours over a six-year period, but it resulted in an instrument that would become Garcia's principal live guitar for 11 years. Tiger's first live performance was at a Grateful Dead concert in Oakland in 1979, and it was played during the last song of Garcia's final performance with the band, at Soldier Field in Chicago in July 1995. He died one month later.

Tiger is an incredible feat of luthiery, tipping the scales at 13.5lb and incorporating exotic tonewoods such as cocobolo for the top and back, with a maple and padauk core. The guitar is resplendent with lavish details from the brass binding to the stunning marquetry and mother-of-pearl inlay work at the rear, framed by quilted maple. The tiger that gives the guitar its name is inlaid behind the tailpiece in mother of pearl on ebony, while the three-piece flame maple and padauk neck is also brass-bound. Garcia's eagle logo features on the headstock fascia and his name is inlaid at the end of the fingerboard.

On the electronic side of things, the guitar's sophisticated switching gave Garcia 12 possible voices to play with – a broad palette for an artist who always painted in technicolor. After Garcia's death, Tiger and Wolf were returned to Doug Irwin, to whom Garcia bequeathed the guitars. Irwin sold them both at auction in 2002, with Tiger selling for $957,500 to guitar enthusiast and owner of American football team the Indianapolis Colts, Jim Irsay. The guitar now takes pride of place in a glass cabinet on the wall above Irsay's desk at Colts HQ, but it makes regular appearances at Jim Irsay Collection live events – free concerts that bring people together through the love of music, very much keeping the Deadhead spirit alive.

'59 GIBSON S/B LES PAUL

KEITH RICHARDS/MICK TAYLOR

The Rolling Stones

Exile on Main St. Burst – 1959 Gibson Les Paul Standard

Les Paul Standards from Gibson's golden era are some of the most desirable electric guitars in the world. Only 1,400 or so were made between 1958 and 1960, and the shipping ledgers from that period went missing when Gibson relocated from Kalamazoo to Nashville in the 1980s. As a result, it can be challenging to trace the history of the guitars when they appear on the market, and those with indisputable provenance are extremely sought after.

These guitars are known colloquially as "Bursts" by collectors and fans – so-called for their vivid red and yellow sunburst paintwork. The red pigment often faded due to UV exposure (sometimes before the guitars had even left the shop window), leaving an amber or lemon hue behind. The most attractive examples are renowned for their intensely flamed maple tops, which shimmer through the paintwork with a three-dimensional quality that changes with the light.

I've been lucky to photograph many Bursts over the years, but it's rare to come across one that has been played by not just one but two iconic guitarists, during the creation of one of the most influential rock albums of all time: *Exile on Main St.* by The Rolling Stones. This Burst was played by both Keith Richards and Mick Taylor during the overdub sessions for the album at Sunset Sound studio in Los Angeles – documented by photographer Jim Marshall's famous portraits from the session.

Outside the studio, the guitar headed out on the road and was used live by Mick Taylor during The Rolling Stones' legendary North American tour in 1972, and for further dates the following year. The guitar left the band along with Mick Taylor in 1974. It was later sold to a guitar shop in London, from which a private collector friend of mine picked it up in the early 1980s, who has kept it ever since.

With such a close association to rock royalty, it would be easy to tuck this guitar into a display case to be revered yet never played again. But this is a beautiful example of a Burst that has been loved and cared for, while still remaining a working instrument. There is something quite special about it and it truly appears to glow. Hairline checking adds a toffee-apple-like quality to the body lacquer, with a distinctive swirl around the bridge pickup's tone knob. Underneath the pickguard, safe from any hint of UV fading, the paintwork maintains a triangle of its original vibrant red hue. Deep fretboard wear marks the paths once traced by the guitar's former owners on songs that will continue to resonate and inspire those who encounter this historic instrument.

Gibson

PINK FLOYD.
LONDON.
VOX
VOLUME
TONE
TONE

DAVID GILMOUR

Pink Floyd

The Black Strat – Fender Stratocaster

In 2019 I was sent to the prestigious Christie's auction house in London to photograph the unveiling of David Gilmour's epically generous guitar auction in aid of environmental law charity, ClientEarth. The highlight of the collection was his iconic Black Strat, which made its first public appearance with Pink Floyd at the 1970 Bath Festival and was then used on many of the band's most-loved songs, including "Money", "Comfortably Numb" and "Shine On You Crazy Diamond".

As a crowd of the world's press jostled for position behind velvet-rope stanchions, the guitar was brought out to a great hubbub. White-gloved handlers presented it to the crowd before placing it delicately on display. Quite the spectacle for a heavily modified old Stratocaster with very few original parts.

Fast-forward a few months and I was in Indiana, sat with the Black Strat in my hands beneath a museum display case containing Jack Kerouac's original manuscript of *On the Road*. Jim Irsay, the guitar's new custodian and collector of pop culture artefacts, had graciously agreed to a magazine feature detailing some of his most important acquisitions. The Black Strat was to be the cover star.

David Gilmour purchased the guitar in 1970 from Manny's in New York to replace another Stratocaster that had been stolen. Originally a sunburst and refinished in black before David bought it, these days you can see glimpses of the factory finish peeking through. Few guitars have been modified more extensively; the neck has been replaced several times, as have the hardware and electronics. After ten years on loan to the Hard Rock Cafe in Dallas, where many eager hands had caused it significant damage, the guitar was returned to David in the late 1990s and it underwent a much-needed restoration, returning to the live stage for high-profile performances such as the Pink Floyd reunion at Live 8, in London, in 2005.

Revered as one of rock's true six-string icons, the Black Strat has captured imaginations, and a staggering $3,975,000 was raised for charity by the sale of this guitar alone. However, David himself never saw the guitar as much more than a working tool, describing it as "just an ordinary Strat that I bought at Manny's". Nevertheless, it became much more than that to the fans.

TONE
TONE

Fender
STRATOCASTER

RORY GALLAGHER

1961 Fender Stratocaster

One of my first guitar photography jobs was at a small storage space in West London crammed full of Rory Gallagher's possessions. At that time, my lighting kit was quite large, so it was with much trepidation that I squeezed it through the walls of cardboard boxes and up a very narrow, very steep ladder into the loft above. Upstairs were seemingly endless shelving units housing Rory's vinyl and cassette collection. It was extensive, just crying out for one of those questionable statistics such as, "laid end-to-end, Rory Gallagher's record collection would reach three times from the Earth to the Moon."

I was to photograph Rory Gallagher's famous heavily worn sunburst Stratocaster for a pull-out poster in *Guitar World* magazine. Although I'd been on many portrait shoots and behind-the-scenes rig tours, I had never seen or photographed an instrument like this before. The sunburst finish had all but worn away and the wood beneath had taken on an oily patina. The back of the guitar was stained with a blueish hue thanks to Rory's love of double-denim, the pickup covers were yellowed and the ridges of the control knobs were thickly congested. They wanted me to photograph this?!

Irish blues legend Rory Gallagher purchased his main guitar, a 1961 Fender Stratocaster, secondhand from Crowley's Music Shop in Cork in 1963, on credit for £100. In midcentury, working-class Ireland, the price might as well have been a million pounds, prompting his mother to despair, "We'll be in debt for the rest of our lives." Claimed to have been the first Stratocaster in Ireland, the story goes that the guitar's previous owner, Jim Conlon of Waterford outfit The Royal Showband, had ordered a red Stratocaster from the USA – presumably inspired by Hank Marvin – but this sunburst model was delivered by mistake. He used the guitar for a year until a replacement arrived, after which he put it up for sale in Crowley's.

Once the guitar was in Rory's hands, its sunburst finish was quickly worn away. This was in part due to extensive playing and the fragility of the lacquer, and also accredited to the high levels of moisture the guitar absorbed. Another theory is that Rory had unusually acidic sweat due to a rare blood type. It certainly didn't help when, in 1966, the guitar was stolen and abandoned for several days in a ditch, in rainy Ireland.

Rory died in 1995. Since then, his brother Donal and nephew Daniel have curated his legacy, occasionally bringing the guitar out for honoured guests. In 2011, Joe Bonamassa used it across two nights at the Hammersmith Apollo, opening both performances with his version of "Cradle Rock".

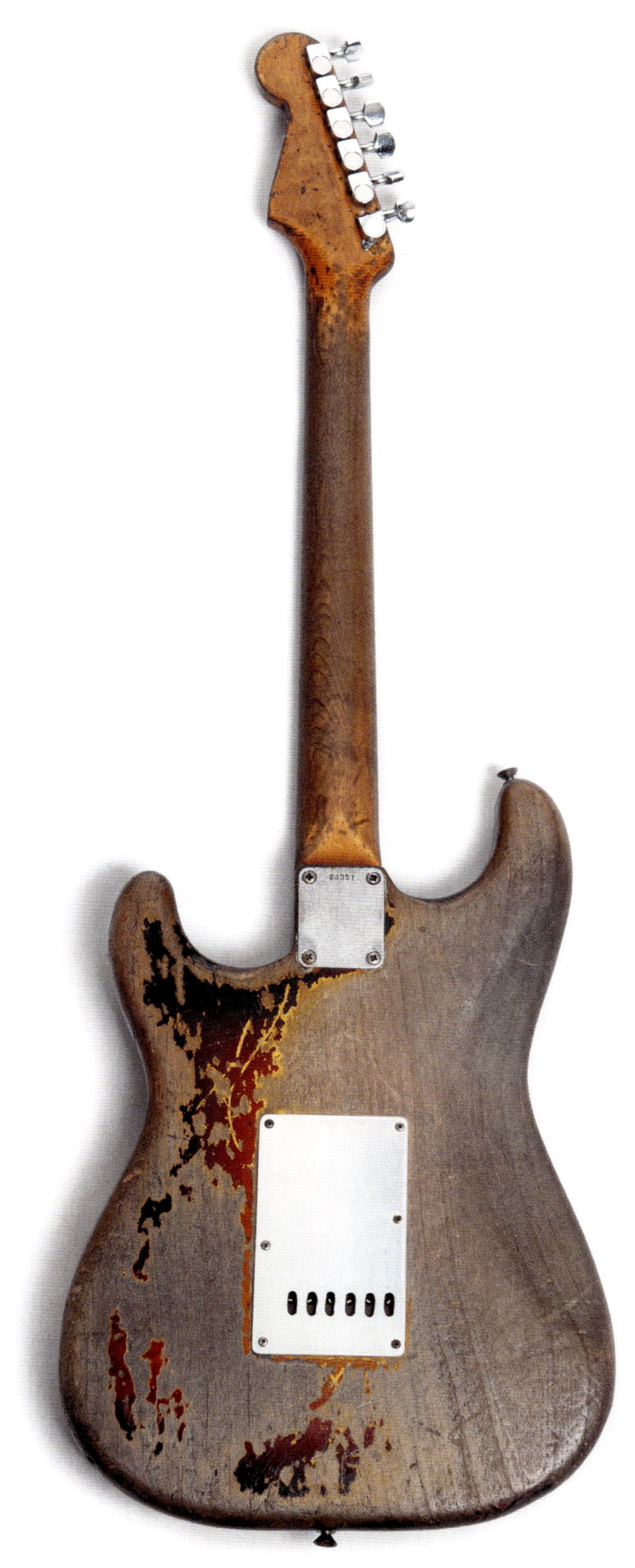

BRIAN RAY

1957 Gibson Les Paul Goldtop

In a mid-century modern Palm Springs hideaway, framed by gently swaying palm trees whispering in the desert breeze, a pink sunset glow begins to fall across a Les Paul-shaped infinity pool. Brian Ray places a brown Lifton case on the original terracotta tile floor and slowly releases the catches. He cracks open the lid to reveal a 1957 Gibson Les Paul Goldtop with a beautiful patina.

Brian purchased the guitar in 1973 from his half-sister's boyfriend, who had bought it in New York from either Manny's or We Buy Guitars – the details are fuzzy now. The boyfriend had paid $550 and sold it on to Brian for $850 – a princely sum in those days, equalling around three months' rent. The Goldtop was instantly a cherished possession, and as a teenager Brian bonded deeply with it. The guitar became a tool to help him express his inner feelings through music when he couldn't find the words.

Brian played the guitar throughout his time as bandleader with Etta James, from "sweaty little gigs" right the way through to the Montreux Jazz Festival in Switzerland. When Brian and Etta toured with The Rolling Stones between 1978 and 1980, the Goldtop came right along with them. Keith Richards, a close friend of Etta James, sat in with the band on several occasions, using Brian's guitar, which was always a thrill.

The guitar has so much character; the action it has seen over the years is evident in the play-wear, alongside the natural ageing of the finish. In places the gold nitrocellulose lacquer is worn down to the wood, and in others it has turned green through oxidization, which creates verdigris when the bronze particles in the paint react with oxygen over time. There's even a repair on the back of the body that seems to have been done in a pinch with chewing gum and never revisited.

When Brian first bought the guitar it had non-original pickups with the covers removed, but he thought they sounded great, and few guitarists cared much for the originality of guitar parts in the 1970s. He only changed the pickups when what was probably a culmination of sweat rotting through the windings finally put them out of action. In the mid-1980s, Brian set about restoring the Goldtop to factory specifications, collecting original parts from all over the world.

For more than 20 years, Brian has played both guitar and bass with Sir Paul McCartney. But naturally protective of the guitar that holds so many wonderful memories for him, Brian has retired the Goldtop from touring. One of the final times he used it in public was at the 2012 Grammy Awards, when he jammed onstage with Sir Paul, Joe Walsh, Dave Grohl and Bruce Springsteen. While Brian continues to rock on, a peaceful retirement in Palm Springs is not a bad way for the Goldtop to bow out of the limelight.

Gibson

DELUXE

RANGEMASTER
TREBLE BOOSTER
BOOST
VOX

BRIAN MAY

Queen

The Red Special

In August 1963, in a small house in Feltham, Middlesex, seven years before the formation of Queen, 15-year-old Brian May and his father, Harold, began a woodworking project that, remarkably, would result in one of the most-heard guitars in the history of recorded music. Constructed mainly from repurposed materials found around the family home, the Red Special is a testament to astounding resourcefulness and ingenuity, and is crammed full of personal touches.

The guitar's neck came from the wood of a 100-year-old fireplace donated by a family friend, which was riddled with woodworm holes that Brian filled with matchsticks. Mrs May's craft supplies seem to have been regularly plundered; the mother-of-pearl inlays were hand-shaped by Brian from buttons he found in his mother's sewing box, and the vibrato arm's tip was crafted from the end of one of her knitting needles. The arm itself started life as a bicycle saddle-bag holder. The original knobs came from an old radio but were later replaced.

Harold and Brian wound the original pickups from scratch, first building a pickup winding machine on which to do so, but the sound wasn't what Brian had hoped for so he purchased a set of Burns Tri-Sonic pickups and opted to use those instead. Six decades and 300 million album sales later, it's hard to argue with the results.

Over the years, the way that Brian plays the guitar has left a unique impression on the Red Special. His use of a British sixpence as a guitar pick has not only created distinctive deep gouges in the pickup covers, but it also leaves a fine layer of copper and nickel dust in the areas between the pickups.

The headstock originally featured Brian's initials but over the years he has continued to personalize the guitar, and a commemorative sixpence from his 1993 *Back To The Light* tour now takes pride of place. Although Brian owns numerous replicas, he still tours and records with the original Red Special to this day.

BURNS
TRI-SONIC

BERNIE MARSDEN

Whitesnake

The Beast – 1959 Gibson Les Paul Standard

In 1974, while playing at London's famous Marquee Club with a hard rock band called Wild Turkey, Bernie Marsden was approached by a man who had found his way backstage, 1959 Les Paul in hand, urging Bernie to play it. Bernie plugged in the guitar and was instantly wowed by how huge it sounded. He used it for the encore, immediately fell in love and asked the guy how much he wanted for it. The price tag of £600 was more than Bernie could afford at the time, but guitarists are ever resourceful when chasing the holy grail, and Bernie traded a couple of guitars until they had a deal.

The man in question had bought the guitar from Free's Andy Fraser, who had bought the guitar from Paul Kossoff, who'd bought it from Eric Clapton... or so the story goes. From then onwards, the guitar that became known as The Beast would be synonymous with Bernie Marsden. His number one throughout his long career, it was famously used to write a string of Whitesnake classics, including "Here I Go Again", which at 8 million radio plays and counting is certainly one of the biggest rock hits of all time.

When Bernie first purchased The Beast it was still a vibrant cherry sunburst but, as with many 1959 Les Pauls, the red pigment faded to leave the guitar with a golden-orange hue. It's a beautiful guitar, with a glimmering flamed-maple top, and although it has a few dings and areas of play-wear, it looks and feels like an instrument that was cherished rather than beaten.

Bernie passed away in 2023, and it was a terrible loss to the guitar community. Over the years we had some enjoyable photoshoots. He was kind and generous with his time and would always make sure you were well looked after when you visited; vegan lemon cake homemade by his wife Fran and lunch in the garden being some favourite memories.

My favourite quote about Bernie was something Joe Bonamassa said in a *Guitar Magazine* feature from 2017: "Underestimate Bernie Marsden at your peril, because as a singer he'll kick your ass, as a player he'll kick your ass, and as a songwriter he'll definitely kick your ass!"

It's so true. Once, when I was shooting some of Bernie's vintage acoustic guitars in his snooker room, he picked one up, perched on a stool and launched into song – a truly fantastic private performance. His playing was impeccable and he had a heck of a voice.

Gibson
Les Paul
MODEL

FRIEDMAN
erosmth
Seymour Duncan
Seymour Duncan

JOE PERRY

Aerosmith

1325 – Made On Earth

It's Valentine's Day, I'm in Las Vegas and I'm about to spend the afternoon with Aerosmith. Inexplicably, I've been upgraded to a luxury suite with chauffeur limo service and a butler who rings my doorbell to check if I need someone to lay out my slippers. As short-notice photoshoots go, it's one of the good ones.

I'm waiting on the gambling floor of the Park MGM to meet my contact, slot machines jingling, the faintly disguised smell of cigar smoke in the air. I'm ushered into the service entrance and led through industrial-looking corridors backstage to the beating heart of the Aerosmith operation. Showtime is in a few hours and we have a lot to get done. Before the magazine cover shoot, it's time to get stuck into the guitar rig. Vegas shows are a tight operation and the crew are eager to run through their checks, so for speed and convenience I'm relegated to using guitar stands. It's not my favourite solution but needs must, and it's a privilege to be here.

Joe Perry has spent half a century in one of the most successful rock bands of all time and it goes without saying that he can own pretty much any guitar he wants – and he certainly has his fair share of the cream of the vintage crop. However, one look around his touring rig tells you that he's a complete gearhead who often chooses more leftfield, luthier-built custom instruments over mainstream brands. It's actually a totally different experience for me because it's impossible to guess what's coming next.

Joe's tech pulls all sorts of crazy things from road-cases, and one guitar in particular stands out. It's named "1325" after 1325 Commonwealth Avenue, Boston – the address of the band's original apartment where the "Bad Boys from Boston" lived together, no doubt in hedonistic excess, between 1970 and 1972. The guitar was made by Brandon Jones, another of Joe Perry's guitar techs and a luthier who builds unique creations under the Made On Earth guitar brand.

The design is based on Aerosmith's original hand-painted tour van, the side of which was emblazoned with their first band logo and a huge portrait of former road manager Mark Lehman, referenced in "Mama Kin" as "bald as an egg at eighteen". During this Las Vegas residency, the van is on display outside the concert venue. It was rediscovered in 2018 by *American Pickers* stars Mike Wolfe and Frank Fritz after it had been left abandoned in the woods 110 miles outside of Boston.

The guitar's fretboard features intricate bone inlays depicting each band member. Brandon Jones chose bone for its visual contrast with the ebony fingerboard. While pondering what material to use, his dog walked in with a bone in her mouth. He promptly ran the bone through a bandsaw, cleaned it up with a belt sander and turned it into inlays. Another unique touch for a one-of-a-kind guitar.

smth
1
3
2
5

62
AEROSMITH
TALENT
erosmith
LET THE MUSIC
RAG DOLL
LAST CHILD
PINK
HANGMAN
SEASONS

Bigsby
PATENT
D169,120

KIRK HAMMETT

Metallica

Factory Black 1959 Les Paul Standard

When it comes to rare guitars, there are unicorns, and then there is a 1959 Les Paul Standard in factory black. May 1958 saw the first cherry sunburst Les Paul Standards leave Gibson's Kalamazoo facility, superseding the metallic "Goldtop" finish that had featured on the model since 1952. The 1,400 or so cherry sunburst Les Pauls made between 1958 and 1960 are considered the most desirable prize by many guitar collectors, but much rarer still are factory black Les Paul Standards from the same era, with only two confirmed to exist.

Black Les Paul Customs, of course, were rather more plentiful. But they were also more expensive. If you couldn't afford one, you either had to get creative with a spray can (bad idea) or place a custom order. However, it seems like only two people ever did, as there are just two known Les Paul Standards that left Kalamazoo with a black finish applied at the factory. Joe Bonamassa owns one of them – a 1960 model nicknamed The Black Burst – and now Kirk Hammett owns the other, possibly the only 1959 Les Paul Standard in factory black in existence.

The guitar came to be when a young jazz musician named Joseph Arena wanted a black Les Paul Custom to match his tuxedo. But the $395 Custom was out of his price range, so instead he placed an order with Gibson for the more affordable Les Paul Standard ($265) with a black finish and Bigsby vibrato. The guitar was ordered through a Sam Ash guitar store in New York State and remained with the family until 2022, when it found its way to Carter Vintage Guitars in Nashville, Tennessee. There it caught the attention of Metallica's Kirk Hammett, another avid vintage collector and a man who can't get enough of black guitars, or vintage Les Pauls in general.

In recent years, Kirk has been the custodian of Greeny, the 1959 Les Paul Standard previously owned by Peter Green and Gary Moore. Despite it being one of the most famous electric guitars in history, Greeny never leaves his side, and he can be seen shredding away on it all over the world with Metallica. But this factory black '59 definitely has more of a metal edge, and it was quickly integrated into Kirk's live setup, appearing on stage almost immediately after he purchased it, and also during Metallica's performance on *The Howard Stern Show*.

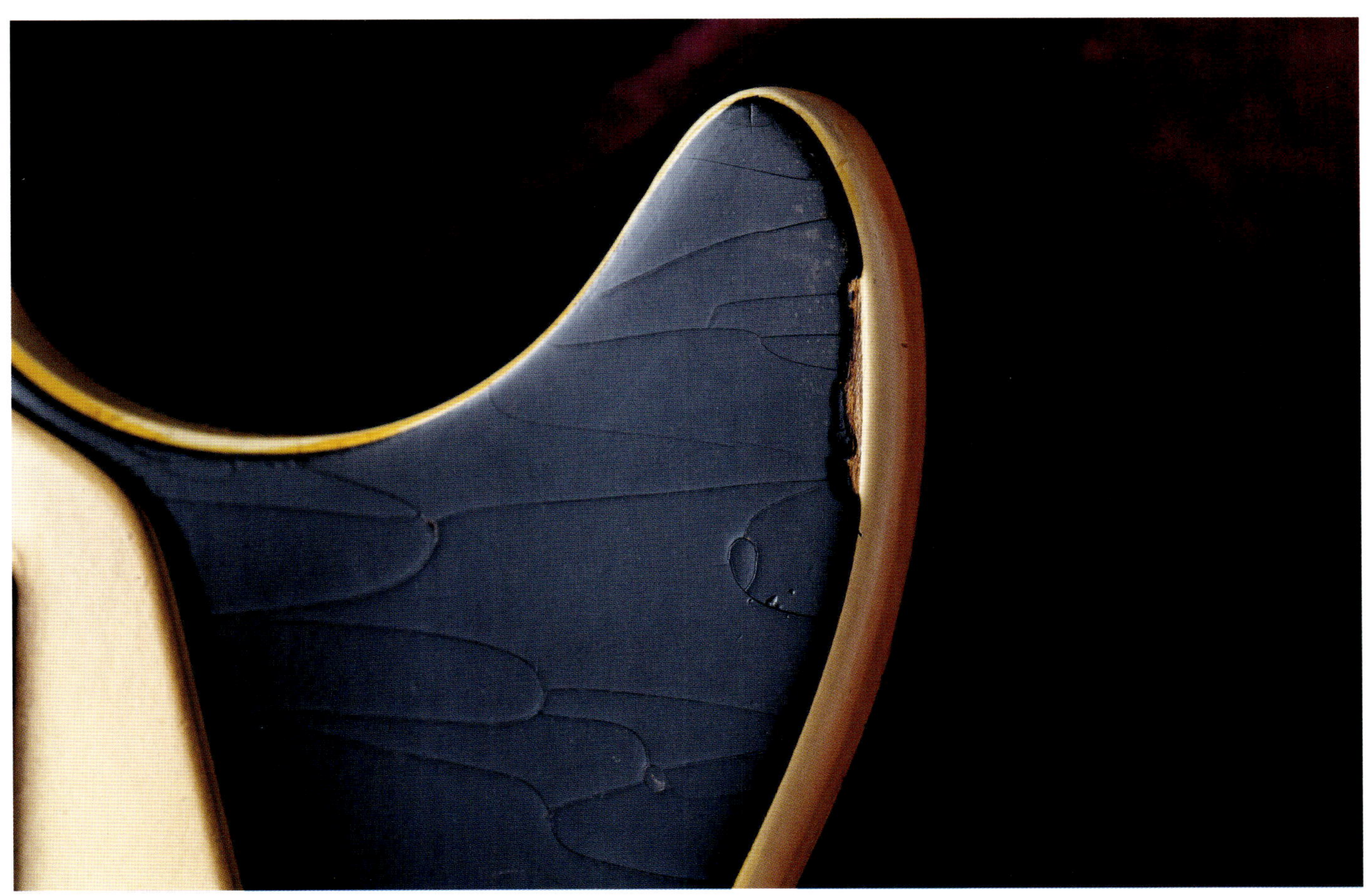

Bigsby
PATENT

EVO

STEVE VAI

Evo – Ibanez JEM

Steve Vai's character in the 1986 movie *Crossroads* might have sold his soul to the devil in exchange for supernatural guitar skills, but when I'm invited into Steve's private backyard studio, thankfully the stakes aren't quite so high. Known as the Harmony Hut, it's a zen-like space with a meditation loft in the eaves and library cabinets full of music and photography books that line the walls. Every inch that isn't devoted to gear is draped in beautiful fabrics. Steve's taste in guitars leans toward the modern rather than vintage, but there are plenty of racks stuffed with old compressors and EQs. It's a warm and cosy sanctuary that no doubt provides a calm, inspiring environment in which to create. Steve is recording a documentary in the adjoining room, and after a quick chat, I'm left alone with several of his most iconic guitars, to enjoy the atmosphere and create a little something of my own.

Steve's number-one guitar, which he has been playing for over 30 years, is an Ibanez JEM signature model named Evo. Steve had been working with Ibanez on designing a new guitar, wanting a JEM model with more of a classic look. Ibanez sent out four production models, completely standard with no modifications, so Steve could start to play them and get a feel for which one he would like to use. On looks alone, he couldn't tell them apart – white bodies, gold hardware, vine inlays – but they all felt subtly different.

He was simultaneously working with DiMarzio on a new pickup design, of which there were four prototypes, each named after a different Harley-Davidson engine: Flathead, Knucklehead, Panhead and Evolution. Evolution was the winner, so Steve had the pickups installed in one of the new Ibanez prototypes and wrote "Evo" on the guitar in order to tell them apart. This quickly became his favourite. "There was something about Evo that I responded to," Steve says on his website. "Even though she was technically exactly like every other production-model guitar, there was something about her touch and sound that moved me."

These days, thanks to Steve's high-octane playing style, Evo is in fragile condition. The guitar has had many necks, and a repair to a substantial crack running right through the body. "Although Evo is just made out of wire and wood, I'm afraid of how much emotional investment I have in her," Steve goes on to admit. "I think when you play an instrument for long enough it becomes an extension of yourself in ways that run deeper than anyone may understand but you. For me, Evo has been the voice of my heart."

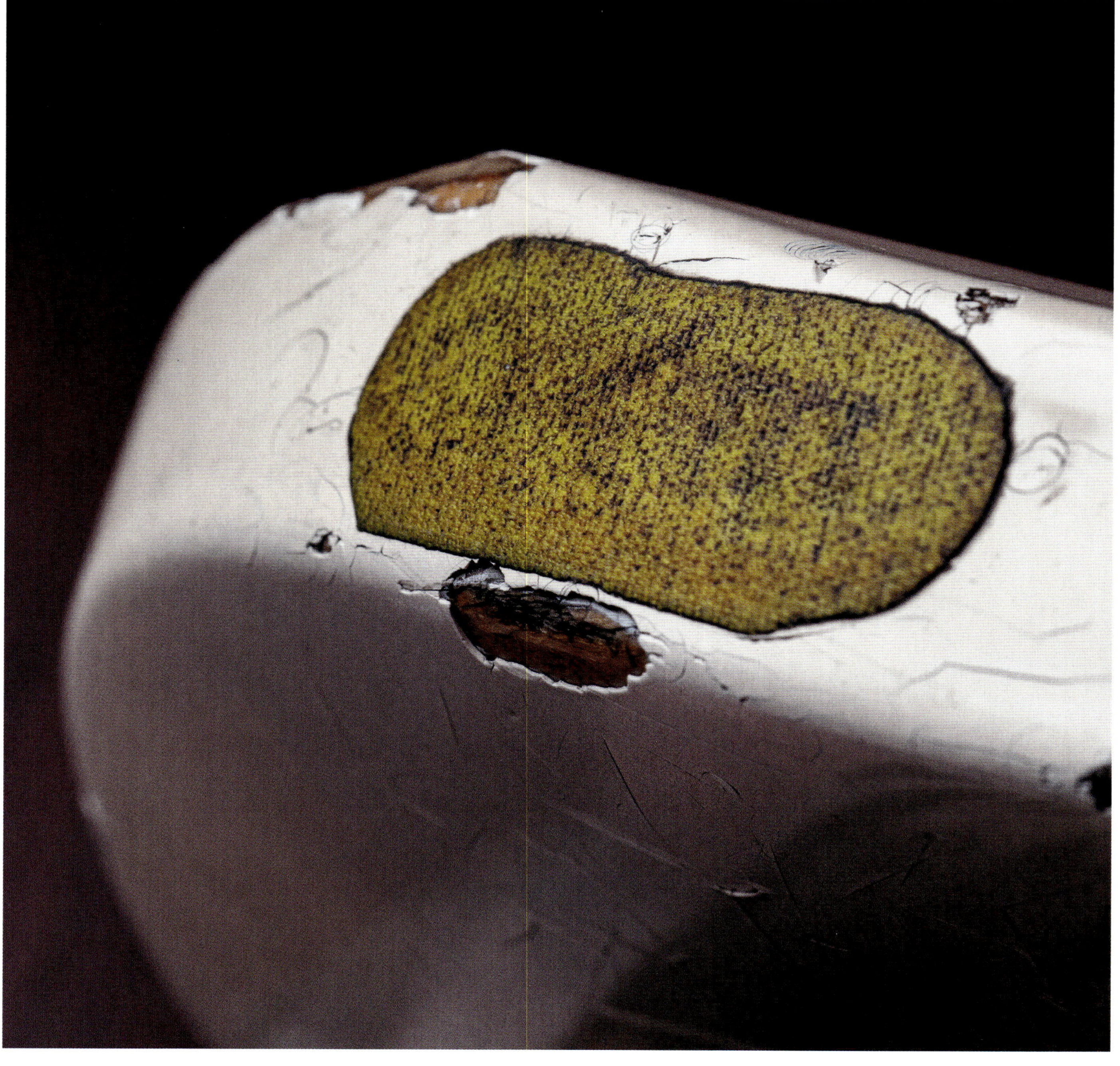

"Everything Is Music"

Ibanez
JEM

RHYTHM
TREBLE
DiMARZIO
Floyd Rose

NEAL SCHON

Journey

"Don't Stop Believin'" – 1977 Gibson Les Paul Pro Deluxe

Love it or hate it, "Don't Stop Believin'" by Journey is a karaoke classic. If you've ever got up on the microphone to sing it, the chances are you've tried and failed to hit those famous high notes.

Journey guitarist Neal Schon taught himself to play guitar by ear as a child while playing along to his record collection. Neal was encouraged by his father, himself an accomplished musician – a tenor sax player and big band leader who wrote arrangements for jazz legends such as Wes Montgomery. By the 1970s, Neal was in his teens and playing the San Francisco clubs when he attracted the attention of not one, but two legendary artists, Carlos Santana and Eric Clapton, both of whom asked him to be in their bands. A tough decision, but in 1971, at the age of just 17, he chose to join Santana.

Two years later, Neal and some other San Francisco musicians, including former Santana keyboard player Gregg Rolie, formed Journey. But it wasn't until the arrival of singer Steve Perry in 1977 that the band really started to take off. Neal used this guitar – a 1977 Les Paul Pro Deluxe – to co-write many of their hits. It was with this guitar that they recorded numerous songs on their breakthrough, nine-times platinum album *Escape*, including "Who's Crying Now", "Stone in Love" and, of course, "Don't Stop Believin'".

For such a successful and enduring song, "Don't Stop Believin'" has a unique structure. The guitar solo arrives inside the first minute and, much like the "midnight train going anywhere" in the lyrics, propels the song forward into an anthem of inspiration that keeps building... until the chorus finally kicks in at the end.

When he used it on the band's famous 1981 *Escape* tour, the Houston leg of which was broadcast by MTV, the guitar still had its neck P-90 pickup. Neal had also added a humbucker at the bridge, and claims he was the first guitarist to fit a Floyd Rose whammy bar and locking nut to a Les Paul. The Ferrari sticker around the back has been in place for many years. Today the guitar sports a DiMarzio twin-blade pickup and a Fernandes Sustainer in the neck position, and Neal's signature in silver ink on the back of the headstock.

"Don't Stop Believin'" has never lacked in popularity, receiving heavy radio play for the past 40 years. But when the cast of TV musical show *Glee* performed the hit on an episode in 2009, the track was reinvigorated, becoming one of the top-selling tracks in iTunes history, bringing the band a whole new generation of fans.

LES PAUL-DELUXE
MADE IN USA
06115596
GIBSON

Floyd Rose
original

DiMARZIO

VOX
EMG
EMG

PRINCE

Yellow Cloud – Andy Beech

By any measure one of the most revered and idiosyncratic musicians of all time, Prince Rogers Nelson was a staggering talent. As comfortable tearing up stages with searing rock guitar solos as he was laying down smooth funk and R&B grooves or penning power ballads, it's hardly surprising that Prince's taste in guitars was eclectic.

Of all Prince's guitars, the Cloud models are comfortably the most iconic. But the origin story of the Cloud and its design is complicated to say the least, and often disputed. The facts go something like this: in 1983, Prince engaged Minnesota-based music store Knut-Koupée to build what is thought to be the first ever Cloud guitar, for use in the movie *Purple Rain*. Dave Rusan was the luthier tasked with the commission and, having once auditioned for Prince's band, he was slightly more qualified than most to interpret exactly what the flamboyant musician wanted in a guitar.

Rusan didn't have much to go on, other than the instruction to replicate a Sardonyx bass designed and built by Jeffrey Levin in New York in the early 1970s. Prince had purchased the bass from Matt Umanov Guitars in New York City, where Levin worked as a guitar repairer. Prince was apparently captivated by the shape, describing it as "very erotic". The Sardonyx featured a scroll design inspired by the Gibson F-style mandolin and an elongated upper horn to aid balance. The result was an instrument with an almost alien appearance.

Rusan replicated the design in guitar form, in white, with gold hardware. Prince loved it so much he ordered several more guitars from Rusan between 1983 and 1985, then further Cloud models were commissioned from luthier Andy Beech, including this yellow version which became Prince's main guitar from around 1988 until 1994, according to his former guitar tech Zeke Clark. Clark stated that this particular model was used all over the world until Prince broke the neck on a French TV show. Clark repaired the neck and installed the Floyd Rose vibrato, which he says was the first Prince ever played. Today the guitar resides alongside numerous other star guitars in the Jim Irsay Collection in Indianapolis.

VOX
EMG
EMG

ERIC CLAPTON

MTV Unplugged – 1939 Martin 000-42

In the 1980s, acoustic guitar had fallen out of favour thanks to the sounds of synth pop and hair metal dominating the airwaves. It was a far cry from the early 70s, when folk-influenced singer-songwriters from the Laurel Canyon scene could be heard on every radio station and acoustic guitar sales were at an all-time high.

In 1989, the first episode of *MTV Unplugged* aired. A new concept for the channel, the show featured musicians performing acoustic versions of their songs and it quickly became a hit format. Having an acoustic side to your repertoire and the skill to create alternative arrangements of your songs became a badge of honour, with many bands incorporating additional instrumentation such as string sections. Suddenly, raucous rock songs took on a new sophistication and seriousness.

The commercial success of the *Unplugged* shows and their spin-off albums resuscitated the acoustic guitar market and attracted a new generation of players. After all, strumming an acoustic guitar and singing along to your favourite songs seems a lot more accessible to a beginner than the intimidating prospect of learning to shred.

Eric Clapton's *MTV Unplugged* moment came in 1992 at Bray Studios in Windsor, England. It was a huge success, featuring an understated reworking of "Layla" and a moving rendition of "Tears In Heaven", his tribute to his young son Conor, who had died in a tragic accident the previous year. Clapton's *Unplugged* album was a huge success, winning three Grammy awards and becoming one of the best-selling albums of all time, with over 26 million sales worldwide. It was a reinvention of sorts for Clapton who, prior to *Unplugged*, had been all about

Fender Stratocasters and Armani suits. Fans relished seeing him return to playing vintage instruments and reconnecting with his musical roots.

During the show, Eric played this 1939 Martin 000-42 on several songs, including "Layla". Like many pre-war Martin guitars, it is beautiful in its simplicity, with an abalone-inlaid Adirondack spruce top, abalone snowflake-inlaid ebony fingerboard, Brazilian rosewood back and sides, and a herringbone backstrip.

In 2004 the guitar sold at auction for $791,500 and is now in the collection of Jim Irsay. You can see it at the free Jim Irsay Collection performances and pop-up museums all over the USA.

TONE

THURSTON MOORE

Sonic Youth

Pre-CBS Fender Jazzmaster

In the early 1980s, grunge was still but a twinkle in Seattle's eye, but over in New York, art rock pioneers Sonic Youth were fusing noise, dissonance and punk energy in ways that would prove hugely influential in the alternative rock scene.

Their approach was revolutionary and the band have long been praised for reimagining the possibilities of rock guitar. In the 1980s, while the poodle-permed world around them was shredding away on neon-pink Kramers, Sonic Youth were modifying old junk-shop guitars and creating non-standard tunings and sounds. This was art rock, with more in common with avant-garde composers than their NYC post-punk peers. At times, the Sonic Youth sound was weird and borderline atonal – which on paper sounds like an acquired taste – but while the aural textures it created were challenging, the music still had a pop instinct at its heart.

These were lean days and the instruments Sonic Youth gravitated towards were cheap and unfashionable. But the band needed guitars that could cope with their extensive and experimental modifications and, when the low-end guitars they picked up in thrift stores began to fall apart, something had to give. After a little success came their way they had more money to spend, so Thurston Moore and fellow Sonic Youth guitarist Lee Ranaldo took a trip to the iconic Manny's Music on 48th Street in Midtown Manhattan.

They noticed a Jazzmaster and recognized it as the same style of instrument played by Television's Tom Verlaine. "That was a selling point right there," Thurston Moore told *Guitar Magazine* in an interview in 2020. But Verlaine and Elvis Costello aside, no one else really cared for Jazzmasters in the early 1980s, so Moore and

Ranaldo picked them up for bargain prices, warmed up the soldering iron and began making changes.

This heavily worn and stripped-down pre-CBS sunburst example was picked up as a backup during Sonic Youth's later years, then promoted to number one status when the band had a large amount of equipment stolen. Although he has owned and modified many Jazzmasters over the years, Thurston insists that he has a "very personal relationship" with the guitars he plays. "I never see them as interchangeable," he says.

Fender

TONE

D# D# A# A# C# D#

RED HOT
D-2
FREEMAN
VOLUME
TONE
TONE

JOHN FRUSCIANTE

Red Hot Chili Peppers

1962 Fender Stratocaster

Sometimes I shoot in a studio. Sometimes in an inspiring location. Sometimes I'm perched on the very edge of a huge concert stage in Texas, the bustle of a road crew wheeling flight cases all around, stage lighting checks blasting intrusive washes of red and blue across my field of vision, as I hastily try to complete the assignment and get the shots before soundcheck starts.

And sometimes, the kick drum begins to thunder – one-two, one-two – and soundcheck starts up anyway, so I find myself being bounced backstage into the only space available for me to shoot in: the back of the gear truck. In this instance, the fire techs proceed to test-launch pyrotechnics nearby almost as soon as I clamber inside. Still, booming explosions aside, it's actually a pretty photogenic place to shoot!

Back in the late 1990s, John Frusciante had rejoined the Red Hot Chili Peppers after a tumultuous period of absence. He only had one guitar – a 1962 Fiesta Red Fender Jaguar – having sold many while battling addiction and losing the rest in a house fire. In true Hollywood style, Anthony Kiedis took Frusciante down to Guitar Center on Sunset Boulevard and bought him this 1962 Fender Stratocaster. It became John's main guitar through the Chili Peppers' resurgence and it can be heard extensively on the albums *Californication* and *By The Way*. He still tours with it today.

It's a beater, for sure. The guitar began life with a glossy three-tone sunburst finish, but this has since worn away dramatically. Even in the hands of a more restrained player, the super-thin nitrocellulose lacquer Fender sprayed on guitars in the 1960s would often wear over time, but here the wear patterns are deep, dramatic gouges that have long since passed through the lacquer into the wood beneath. Over the years, Frusciante has made a few modifications, switching out the pickups and tuners, but the guitar remains mostly original. A true workhorse.

RED HOT
D-2

Fender

TONE

DYNAMIC
Fender
VIBRATO
PAT. NO.

KURT COBAIN

Nirvana

"Smells Like Teen Spirit" – 1969 Fender Competition Mustang

The most important guitar icon of my generation was undoubtedly Kurt Cobain. I can vividly remember hearing Nirvana's *Nevermind*, an album that changed everything, on a creaky cassette that made its way around my group of school friends. Stretched and overplayed the tape may have been, but the opening bars of "Smells Like Teen Spirit" were as revelatory then as they are today: raw, visceral, energetic. And the video! Still arresting and utterly irresistible to a teenager – a high-school pep rally that descends into chaos with a screaming Kurt leading the riot, his racing-striped 1969 Fender Mustang slung low across his body.

Many years later the guitar sold at auction for an astounding $4.5 million to Indianapolis Colts owner Jim Irsay, with a considerable portion of the proceeds of the sale donated by the Cobain family to Irsay's own Kicking The Stigma foundation, which seeks to support mental health organizations. I had worked with the Jim Irsay Collection previously, so I put the call out to my contact there, Larry C. Hall, the collection's wonderful and enthusiastic Vice President of Special Projects and Historical Affairs. A few weeks later I found myself once again making the not-inconsiderable journey from London to Indianapolis to meet the guitar in person.

For the photoshoot, I wanted to evoke the spirit and low-budget aesthetic of the "Smells Like Teen Spirit" music video. Shot on a soundstage in Los Angeles, the high-school gymnasium was created from the barest of bones: draped canvas sheets hung in the background, and bright-red duct tape marked out a basketball court on the floor. This was easy to recreate, but not wanting to compromise the quality of the lighting, I said goodbye to the warm, fuzzy tungsten haze of the video. After all, the guitar had never before been seen in such extensive detail and I wanted to do justice to all its dents and bruises.

Although the guitar was reportedly one of Kurt's most beloved instruments, frustration with his onstage sound at a show in Texas in 1991 saw him use the Mustang to bludgeon a mixing desk, causing the circular gouges you can see on the body, as well as damage to the neck join. Chipped paintwork, mysterious rust-coloured stains and even a cigarette burn tell the story of a short but intense period of creativity amid turmoil.

You would be forgiven for thinking the colour of the guitar was Lake Placid Blue, but official Fender literature from the late 1960s describes the Mustang's finish as Competition Burgundy. Though it originally had purple body and headstock edges, these quickly faded. Kurt's guitar now has a greenish tint, but a chip in the headstock paintwork reveals the original vibrant colour below.

Kurt Cobain only owned this guitar for a short time before he died. However, thanks to the cultural impact of "Smells Like Teen Spirit", as Larry rightly states, "Kurt created a seismic shift in how people listened to music, dressed, and lived their lives."

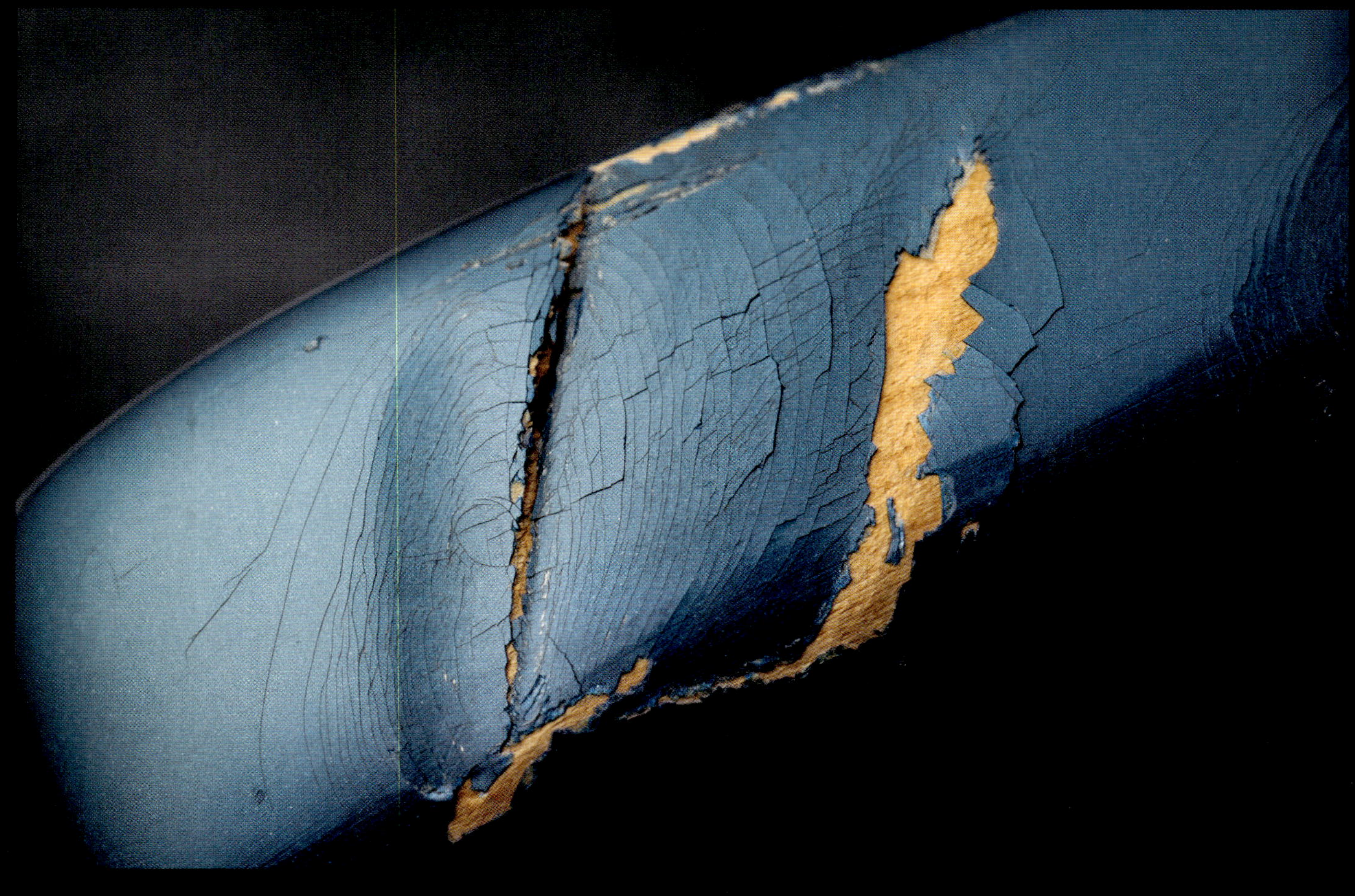

DYNAMIC
Fender
VIBRATO
PAT. NO.

Fender

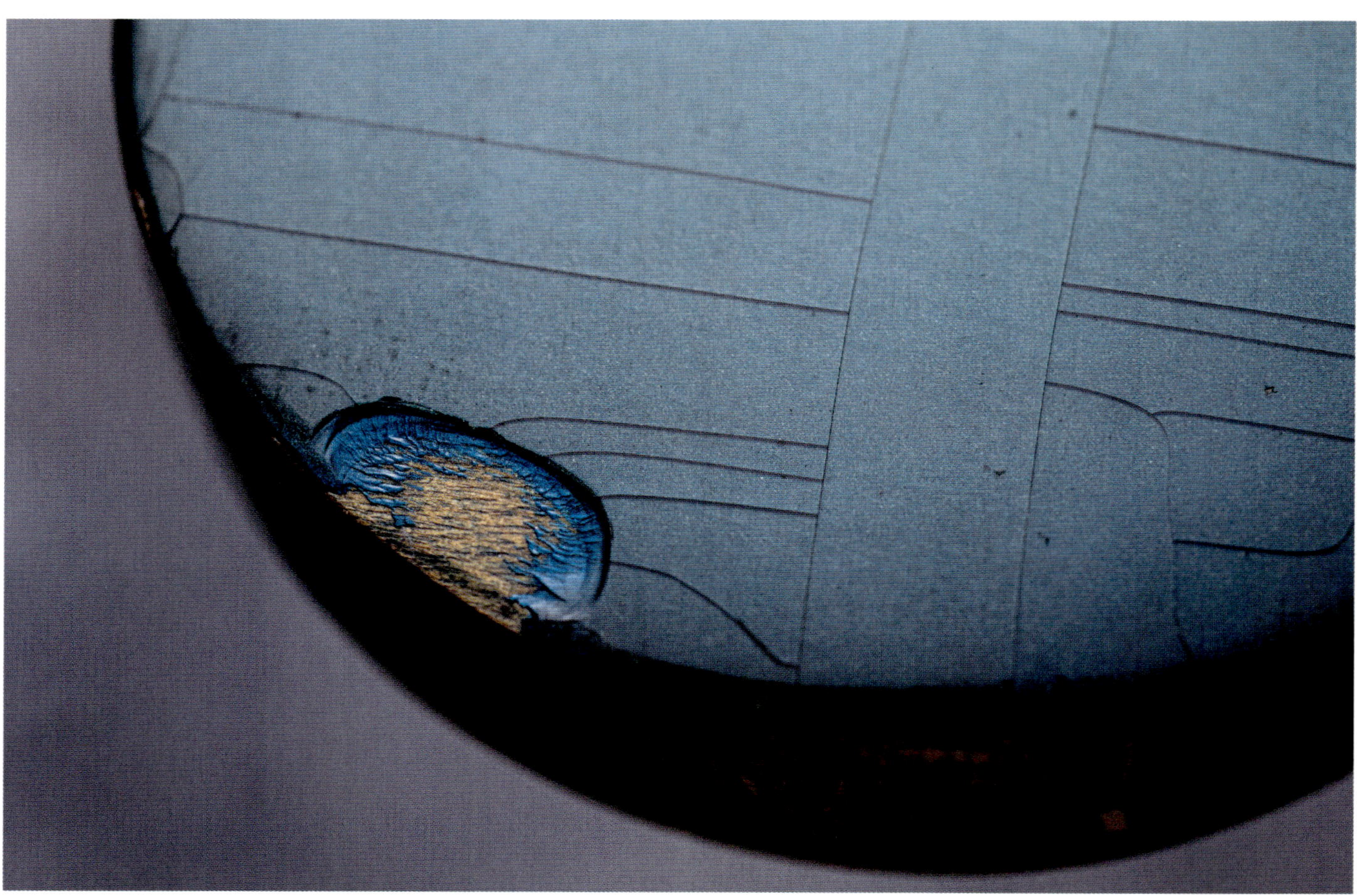

Fender
DYNAMIC

Marsh
EMG
VOLUME
VOLUME
Licensed Under Floyd Rose Patent

TOM MORELLO

Rage Against The Machine

Arm The Homeless

Even casual fans of Rage Against the Machine will undoubtedly be familiar with this guitar – a striking Frankenstein's monster of an instrument that has been Tom Morello's number one for over 30 years. It's a testament to an artist being more than the sum of their tools that, despite playing this guitar on all of his studio albums and at thousands of live shows, it's an instrument that Tom Morello has never been happy with. I visited Tom's home studio in Los Angeles to see it for myself.

In 1986, when Tom first moved to Hollywood, he wanted a custom-built guitar inspired by his shred heroes. With his first pay cheque, he went to a local music store and spec'd out what he thought was his ideal guitar, choosing all of the parts. Not being a luthier and having no real idea what he was doing, Tom admits that the results were terrible. Over the next few years, he tore apart the guitar entirely until all that remained from the original build was the body that you see today.

The guitar saw many necks come and go, until Tom eventually settled on a Kramer-style neck with a "hockey stick" headstock that he found in a rejects bin in a guitar shop on Santa Monica Boulevard. The electronics were changed several times before landing on a set of EMG pickups, and the guitar even sports a Fathead – a brass plate added to the back of the headstock to add more sustain, which Tom says didn't work but he left it on anyway.

Finally, he gave up. Rather than continue to chase the ever-elusive "perfect guitar", Tom decided to create with what he had, embracing the sounds available to him and using that palette to make music – something he described as "very liberating". It's possibly not what the insatiable tinkerers of the guitar world want to hear, but Tom came to realize that music comes from the creativity and artistry of the player wielding the instrument, not the other way around.

One of the key features of the Arm The Homeless guitar that he used to shape his sound was the toggle switch on the lower horn, in conjunction with the individual pickup volume controls. As the de facto DJ in Rage Against The Machine, Tom was responsible for creating turntable-style "scratching" effects. With the volume control for one of the pickups rolled all the way off and the other on 10, the toggle switch becomes an on/off switch – or "killswitch" – which allowed him to create some of the stuttering staccato effects that became a trademark of his sound.

As for the hippos? These were hand-painted by Tom, and "Arm The Homeless" was scrawled across the body shortly before Rage Against The Machine played their first ever headline show at the Whisky a Go Go. Tom enjoyed the juxtaposition of the provocative slogan with the smiling cartoon hippopotamuses – a hippolitical statement, if you will.

Licensed Under Floyd Rose Patents

EMG
VOLUME
VOLUME
TONE

FATHEAD
U.S. PAT.# 4,840,102
TM

JEFF
BUCKLEY

JEFF BUCKLEY

1983 Fender USA Telecaster

Even before his tragic passing in 1997, Jeff Buckley's music had a painful sense of poignancy that is still difficult to put your finger on. The romanticism of his almost supernatural sweeping vocals, achingly beautiful but never overwrought, was matched by his considerable ability as a guitarist.

Although he played several guitars during his short career, this 1983 Fender USA Telecaster was his main instrument both live and in the studio. The Telecaster originally belonged to Janine Nichols, a photographer friend who loaned it to Jeff in 1991 after his New York City apartment was broken into and his guitar stolen. Janine had replaced the original white pickguard with a chrome one in homage to Chrissie Hynde. The guitar was in almost as-new condition when he received it, with a slightly stiff action, so Jeff had some work done on it to improve playability. He evidently bonded with it; it featured on all of his most important recordings, live tours and the intimate coffee-house shows he always felt drawn to.

In late 1996, after the success of *Grace*, Jeff had taken a step back and returned to playing those anonymous cafe gigs that seemed to give his music a sense of purpose. In a message penned to his fans, he explained in his own words how it was playing those smaller shows that allowed him to explore his music and what it meant to him. Performing in front of an audience that didn't necessarily know him gave Jeff the luxury to take risks, to surrender to his music, even to fail. "I loved it then and missed it when it disappeared," he wrote. "All I am doing is reclaiming it."

In early June the following year, Jeff was ready to record again and waiting in

Memphis for his band to arrive to finish the upcoming album. He sat on the shore of the Mississippi River with a friend, a radio and a guitar. Singing. Laughing. Spontaneously, he walked into the water, fully clothed, and swam out under the Wolf River bridge, singing the chorus to Led Zeppelin's "Whole Lotta Love". A boat passed, the friend scrambled to move the radio and the guitar away from the waves thrown up on the bank by the wake of the boat. When he turned back to the Mississippi, Jeff Buckley was gone forever.

At Jeff's memorial in August 1997 the guitar was displayed on stage next to the urn that contained his ashes. After which, his mother returned the guitar to Janine. She later sold the guitar with the wish that it would continue to make music with another artist and, after bouncing through a few private collections, it has now found a home with Matt Bellamy of Muse, who is determined to honour Janine's wish.

Fender®
TELECASTER
MADE IN USA
SERIAL NUMBER E 316334

JEFF
BUCKLEY

VOLUME
VOLUME
B SIDE LAB

RIVERS CUOMO

Weezer

Mei – Warmoth

A Harvard graduate who sometimes prefers to travel around the country to concerts by public transport rather than on a tour bus, Rivers Cuomo is an astoundingly prolific songwriter and every bit the awkward, somewhat reluctant rock star. Of all the guitars in this book, his is probably the most accessible, and certainly the easiest for eager fans to recreate.

When Weezer exploded onto the alternative rock scene in 1994 with their self-titled debut (aka *The Blue Album*), frontman Rivers' knack for penning powerchord-driven pop hits overshadowed his skill as a guitarist. But make no mistake, Rivers Cuomo can *shred*. Indeed, his choice of stage guitars over the years – mainly hardtail Strats assembled from Warmoth parts, with high-output bridge humbuckers – betrayed his early glam metal aspirations, owing plenty to the hotrod guitar culture pioneered by Eddie Van Halen.

His first Warmoth – Sonic Blue with a tortoiseshell pickguard – was assembled in 1993 after the completion of *The Blue Album*. It became iconic during the band's rise to fame but was retired around 2000 due to a split in the body, with the pickups, hardware and neck installed on a new body. This was eventually retired too, with "Mei" taking over live duties ever since.

Another trusty Warmoth S-type, this time in Seafoam Green and covered in stickers gifted to Rivers by fans, Mei is named after a character in the anime classic *My Neighbour Totoro*. Mei is often confused with Satsuki, another stickered Warmoth in Sonic Blue that Rivers uses as a backup.

I photographed Mei in late 2017 on Weezer's *Pacific Daydream* tour in Manchester. Despite it being his main live guitar, Rivers wasn't precious about it, and he was happy for it to be placed on the stage floor for a quick photoshoot before soundcheck. Thanks to the stickers, it's a touching piece of ever-evolving fan art, and one that feels very personal and almost low-key for the lead singer of a band that has sold over 35 million albums worldwide.

VOLUME
VOLUME

JAMES DEAN BRADFIELD

Manic Street Preachers

Faithful – 1990 Gibson Les Paul Custom

This white 1990 Gibson Les Paul Custom owned by James Dean Bradfield of the Manic Street Preachers takes me right back to the beginning of my creative journey, listening to the Manics on cassette tape through screeching, loud, tinny headphones as I rode the bus to college, where I studied photography.

The band and I are from the same small town of Blackwood in the South Wales Valleys – think long terraces of red-brick miners' houses along steep hillsides. The college was on the road out of the Valleys; a surprisingly artsy refuge set between three mountains clad with larch trees – beautiful despite the surrounding area still bearing the scars of a coal-mining industry that was once the lifeblood of the region. But by the time I was riding the 151, the Manics had long since become superstars.

Loud, punky, literate and energetic, the Manics had a lot to say. They were the first band I listened to who were making more than music, they were making a statement. And making a statement was making art. Knowing that art came out of the tiny hometown that felt so stifling at 16 years old really resonated with me as I began to find my own creative voice through photography.

James bought this guitar from Macari's on Denmark Street – the historic street in London's West End where The Rolling Stones recorded their early singles, the Sex Pistols rehearsed and aspiring guitar heroes would go to gawk at vintage instruments in the guitar shops that lined the kerbs. It was 1990 and the Manic Street Preachers had just signed their first record deal. What else would a fan of the Pistols and The Clash choose other than a white Les Paul Custom?

Featuring on all of their studio albums, the guitar came to be known as "Faithful" – perfectly fitting given that the neck has been snapped on three occasions (twice on longhaul flights and once by Manics' bassist and lyricist Nicky Wire) but, happily, it's been resurrected every time. The pickups have been replaced but otherwise the guitar has remained much the same throughout James' career. Where the paint is worn through on the back you can see the signature of one of the band's early heroes: Steve Jones of the Sex Pistols, who signed the guitar for James when they played at the same festival in Belgium.

I photographed Faithful at the Manics' private studio, in a traditional Welsh stone cottage in the countryside overlooking the River Usk. From the outside it's pretty but unassuming. Step beyond the porch, though, and you are greeted by a huge mixing desk that once resided at the legendary Rockfield Studios.

It's a pleasure to encounter the guitar in such familiar and humble surroundings, but the image that endures of James with this guitar is that of a rock icon – headlining huge festivals and stadium shows, leading the crowd in ferociously intelligent, politically charged songs perfectly disguised as anthemic pop singalongs.

RHYTHM
TREBLE

VOL
VOL
TONE
TONE

NOEL GALLAGHER

Oasis

1980s Epiphone Riviera

I'm from the lucky generation whose primary school discos were soundtracked not with bubblegum pop hits or Ibiza trance remixes, but instead with the jangly guitars and melodic regional accents of mid-nineties Britpop. As I bopped away to "Don't Look Back In Anger", I don't think I ever could have imagined that years later I'd be getting up close and personal with the guitar that featured on such an era-defining track.

Noel and Liam Gallagher, the battling Mancunian brothers from one of the UK's biggest bands since The Beatles, provided both the soundtrack and aesthetic of 1990s Britain. If the enduring image of Liam is parka-clad, swaggering up to the microphone with his hands clasped behind his back, then Noel is standing stage left, with the curved body of an Epiphone semi-acoustic guitar, coolly observing a sea of thousands singing his songs back to him.

"I wanted to start playing Epiphones because of The Beatles," Noel told Gibson ahead of a 2023 exhibition showcasing his guitars at the British Music Experience in Liverpool. "I didn't know anything about guitars then. They looked good, they felt good, I could make them sound good. I'm a songwriter, not a guitar player. I'm not one of those people who can sit in a guitar shop and play lots of things. I will literally play an E chord, and if it sounded great and felt good, I would have just said, 'Yeah, I'll take it.'"

The Epiphone Riviera that Noel used throughout the *Morning Glory* era is an early 1980s Japanese model in Wine Red. It was used during the recording sessions for (*What's The Story*) *Morning Glory?*, appeared in the video for "Don't Look Back In Anger" and on stage at the band's 1995 Glastonbury Festival headline performance.

More than any other of Noel's guitars, this Riviera singlehandedly caused an enormous upturn in sales for Epiphone during the second half of the 1990s. In every music pub and nightclub in the land you saw bands take to the stage with Beatle haircuts, anoraks and Epiphone guitars. Guitar music had been democratized; dragged out of the left-field into the tabloids, onto football terraces and into the popular consciousness.

Epiphone

VOL.
TONE
VOL.
TONE

Foo Fighters
Tone-Master
NO.5
INPUT
VOLUME
TREBLE
BASS
MID
FENDER MUSICAL INSTRUMENTS
MADE IN U.S.A.

DAVE GROHL

Foo Fighters

1967 Gibson Trini Lopez Standard

On a suffocating day in the San Fernando Valley, I arrive at an unassuming street in North Hollywood to visit Studio 606 – the Foo Fighters' LA base – to get better acquainted with a guitar Dave Grohl has owned for 30 years and describes as "the sound of the Foo Fighters".

Tucked away in a quiet corner of the complex is the band's private rehearsal room, but to get there we first must journey through their recording studio, then their expansive gear lock-up crammed from floor to cavernous ceiling with guitar cases, elaborate stage props and an entire wall of amps. From there, we traverse corridors lined with pinball machines, skateboards and all sorts of fun memorabilia, eventually ending up in a cosy, down-to-earth space reminiscent of, well... every other rock band's rehearsal room. Miles of trailing black cables, the clutter of microphone and lyric stands, Persian rugs littered with drumstick splinters from a recent rehearsal – even without an audience, it's clear the band plays hard.

Dave talks me through the main guitar that he has used on every Foo Fighters record – the 1967 Gibson Trini Lopez Standard he purchased back in 1992 or 1993 when he was still in Nirvana. He found the guitar at a store in Bethesda, Maryland, and thought it was a little quirky, kind of like a Gibson ES-335 but with diamond-shaped f-holes and a different headstock design. At that time he was unfamiliar with Trini Lopez, the trailblazing Hispanic musician and actor who scored chart hits and hung out with the Rat Pack, but the guitar called to him.

Dave explained to me that he approaches playing the guitar as though it were a drum kit. The sixth string is the kick drum, the fourth and fifth strings are the snare, and the high strings are the cymbals. It seems such an unconventional approach to playing and writing guitar music, but it obviously comes naturally to one of the world's greatest rock drummers.

While you'd expect someone who attacks the guitar with such percussive physicality to wreak havoc on his instruments, Dave's number one Trini Lopez is still in beautiful condition. Long hairline cracks of lacquer checking run through the cherry red finish, the binding has yellowed and there are a few dings and scuffs, but the guitar is ageing gracefully. And it's clearly still a hit with a man who has been in two of the biggest rock bands of all time.

FOO FIGHTERS
rshall

Gibson

JOE BONAMASSA

PJ – 1958 Gibson Les Paul Standard

Through his love for collecting vintage guitars, blues-rock virtuoso Joe Bonamassa has popularized the term "guitar safari". But what does it mean? A guitar safari is best defined as the act of going on an expedition to seek out a rare vintage guitar "in the wild". And, if you're going to go on safari, it might as well be in South Africa.

In Cape Town in 2021, a family walked into a small music store with a guitar to sell after its owner, their great-grandfather, had passed away. The brown case alone was a giveaway that it wasn't any ordinary guitar. Knowing they had something special on their hands, the store put in a call to John Shults of True Vintage Guitar, a young guitar dealer from Alabama making a name for himself on a global scale.

John immediately knew this guitar was special and he turned to the king of the guitar safari, Joe Bonamassa, to pitch a deal. Joe couldn't resist, so John embarked upon an adventure to bring the guitar back to the USA. As with all great adventures, the trip from Birmingham, Alabama, to Cape Town was a challenge. Even when he'd successfully negotiated the deal, pandemic-era flight cancellations meant that the journey home took over 40 hours, connecting in Doha, Qatar – over 4,000 miles in the wrong direction.

But the guitar was worth every minute of the trip. PJ – nicknamed for the handwritten label on the case – is a stunning example of an early sunburst Les Paul Standard from 1958. Bursts manufactured in 1958 are the rarest examples simply because greater quantities were made in 1959 and 1960. PJ has a striking cherry sunburst finish, still vibrant and unfaded, on an un-bookmatched maple top with vivid flame. The nickel hardware is tarnished but this just serves to give the guitar a desirable patina, and it has clearly been well played over the years.

While PJ has been added to Joe Bonamassa's expansive collection, he's not the sort of collector to lock his guitars away. Joe takes his Bursts out on the road and treats them like working musical instruments, in an uncompromising pursuit of tone. So whether it's the Royal Albert Hall or Red Rocks Amphitheatre, you might catch PJ at a live show near you.

Gibson
Les Paul
MODEL

JACK WHITE
The White Stripes
1964 Montgomery Ward Airline

Airlines. They feed back. They complain. They possess wild personalities, or personality disorders, of their own. To play one is to have a constant conversation, sometimes an argument. Or, as Jack White puts it in the 2008 documentary *It Might Get Loud*, a fight: "Pick a fight with it – that's what you gotta do. Pick a fight with it and win the fight." If anyone could wrestle this thing into something resembling submission, it's Jack White.

Airline guitars were manufactured in Chicago by Valco between 1958 and 1968 and sold via Montgomery Ward, the US catalogue and department store. They were deliberately low budget and designed for beginners – cheaply made from "Res-O-Glas", aka fibreglass, the front and back body sections were held together by a refrigerator gasket. Exhibiting the same spirit of mid-century futurism found in fibreglass-bodied Corvettes of the era, the influence of automotive design is clear to see in the Airline's smooth but angular lines.

As a guitar, the Airline is not without limitations and quirks, having all the sonic peculiarities you'd expect from an instrument made from two pieces of plastic held together by a strip of rubber. It's a bit weird, but Jack White likes weird.

The White Stripes, The Raconteurs, The Dead Weather, Third Man Records, even furniture upholstery – Jack White is undeniably a creative powerhouse. Never afraid to experiment, innovate or collaborate, and an advocate of analogue in all its forms, Jack seems to thrive in the creative space between self-imposed limitations, so it is no wonder that he found artistic fulfilment in battling this lo-fi contraption.

This Airline was Jack White's main guitar throughout the ten years in which The White Stripes were active. Bought for less than $200 – probably chosen in part because its red and white colour scheme matched the band's tightly controlled visual identity – it would feature on songs that became garage-blues classics such as "Fell In Love With A Girl", "Ball And Biscuit" and "The Hardest Button To Button".

Although he's an artist who has always been committed to a strong aesthetic, Jack White's music feels like it comes from the soul, and in Jack's hands the Airline is a raw conduit for that emotion. Conclusive proof that you don't need high-tech gear or expensive equipment to sound good – all you need is the music.

TONE

MATT BELLAMY

Muse

DeLorean – Manson Guitar Works

When Muse were beamed back from the future to 1999, it was a timely injection of eccentric British rock music into the charts. Frontman Matt Bellamy fired screaming space rock with stratospheric vocals across the airwaves, bringing a complexity and operatic drama to mainstream rock that hadn't been seen since Queen's 1970s heyday.

After the success of the debut Muse album, *Showbiz*, Matt approached local luthier Hugh Manson and asked him to build a visually striking custom guitar capable of keeping up with his idiosyncratic guitar playing. Growing up in nearby Teignmouth, Matt had been visiting Manson's Exeter shop for years, and was lucky to have a world-renowned guitar builder on his doorstep; Manson had created custom instruments for Led Zeppelin bassist John Paul Jones among others.

Taking visual inspiration from the iconic time-travelling DeLorean from *Back To The Future*, Matt's guitar was to be stuffed full of technology and effects, encased in an industrial-looking, aluminium-plated poplar body. Initially, Hugh Manson thought the plating would be a "nightmare" to polish, however, a chance visit from Matt when the guitar was in a rough and unfinished state, complete with file marks, saved him the trouble – Matt loved the aesthetic.

Today, thanks to Matt's aggressive playing style, the body has numerous additional dents and gouges. There's also a hefty chunk of bird's eye maple missing from the end of the headstock following an onstage incident – Matt is well known for his energetic stage performances and is not averse to smashing his equipment in the heat of the moment.

The DeLorean was used extensively on Muse tours in the early 2000s, and featured in some of their most popular music videos, including "Hyper Music", "Butterflies and Hurricanes", "Dead Star" and "Stockholm Syndrome". With the circuits from ZVEX Fuzz Factory and MXR Phase 90 stompbox effects integrated in the guitar, it kickstarted a copycat craze among more experimental guitar-playing fans, who began retrofitting effects into the bodies of their own instruments.

Since it was retired from live use in 2005, the DeLorean has seen a few changes, most noticeably the original Kent Armstrong Motherbucker in the bridge position being swapped out to facilitate different sounds. It currently features a Bare Knuckle P-90. Still a favourite instrument, the original DeLorean's body silhouette provided the blueprint for nearly all of the Manson Matt Bellamy models that would follow. Owning more than 50 custom Manson instruments, Matt liked them so much he bought the company, becoming a majority shareholder in Manson Guitar Works in 2019.

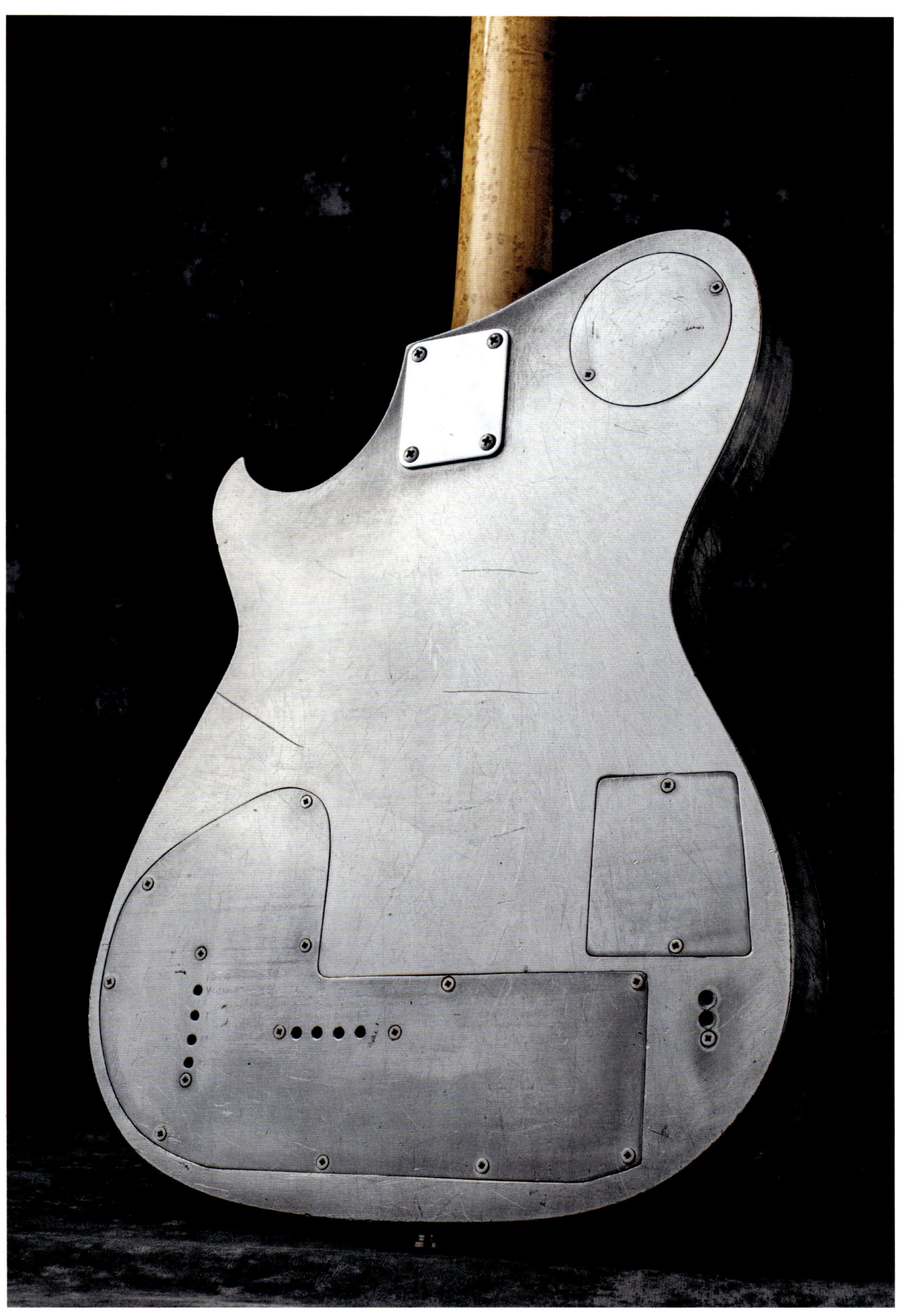

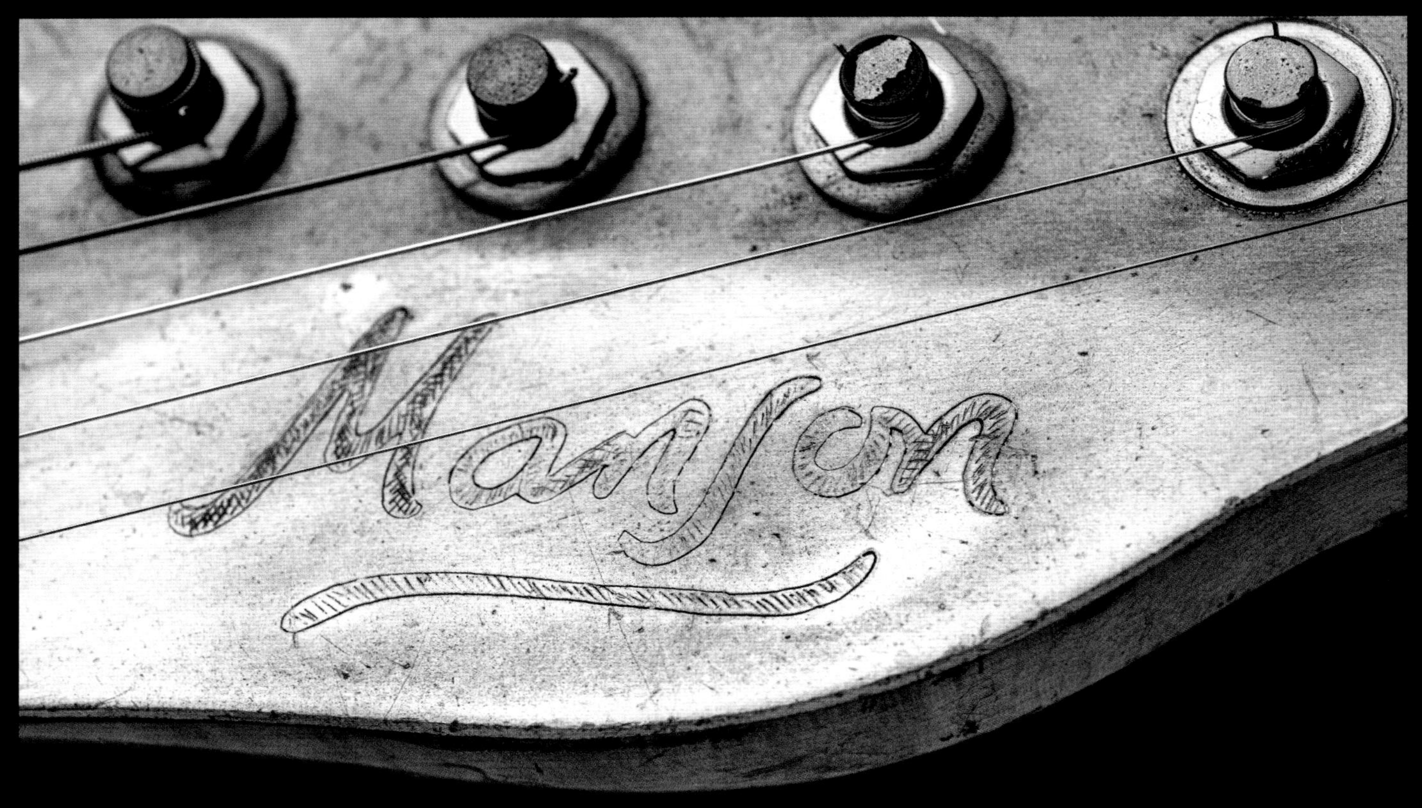
Manson

RHYTHM

JASON ISBELL

Red Eye – 1959 Gibson Les Paul Standard

Jason Isbell grew up in Alabama in a musical family where almost everyone played guitar. His grandfather was a Pentecostal preacher and, when Jason was around seven years old, he began to teach him how to play, starting on the mandolin due to his smaller hands, then progressing to the guitar.

They would play gospel and bluegrass together, but as a reward, his grandfather would treat him to some blues, tuning the guitar to an open chord and playing it on his lap with a pocket knife. Although he's best known as a Southern rock artist, Jason's first love was the blues. After purchasing a Robert Johnson collection from a local record store, his grandfather recorded it onto cassette for him, removing all the songs he considered to be vulgar in the process. He played the tapes until they wore out.

Jason's first ever guitar was a Les Paul copy gifted to him by his uncle, so it's fitting that now his most beloved guitar is the gold standard of Les Pauls. "Red Eye" was previously owned by Ed King, Lynyrd Skynyrd guitarist and co-writer of the Southern rock anthem "Sweet Home Alabama". King bought the guitar in the early 1980s and played it until he passed away in 2018. King's widow Sharon took several of his instruments into Carter Vintage Guitars in Nashville and Jason was invited to demo them. He fell in love with Red Eye before he'd even plugged it in.

Red Eye is so called because of the unfaded section of red paint beneath the pickup selector switch. Back in the late 1950s, Les Paul Standards shipped with a cardboard hang-tag on the switch. The unstable nature of the red pigment in the guitar's finish meant that the colour would fade when exposed to UV light in shop windows, except for the areas protected by either the plastics or the hang-tag, which remain a vibrant red.

Red Eye is close to pristine, with even the headstock corners still possessing a sharp, clean edge. However, as a guitar that sees regular stage use, it has been fully refretted, and the original tuners have been replaced with more robust reproductions. Jason also switched out the tailpiece because he prefers to top-wrap his strings and didn't want to scratch the original.

I get my moment with Red Eye upstairs in the hallowed halls of the Ryman Auditorium in Nashville during one of Jason's annual residencies with his band, The 400 Unit. For someone who grew up playing gospel with his grandfather, it's apt that his spiritual home as a musician would be an old church. Formerly known as the Union Gospel Tabernacle, it's a humble place steeped in Southern musical history, with original wooden floors and whitewashed brick walls. But wherever you see Jason playing, he's likely to have Red Eye by his side. As he admitted in an interview for Gibson TV, "My wife says I would be sitting out in a tent in the middle of a field with just this guitar and one last can of beans at the end of the world."

Gibson
Les Paul
MODEL

1 2
NORMAL
VOLUME
TREBLE
BASS
VIBRATO
Fender

PHOEBE BRIDGERS

Danelectro 56 Baritone

I have fifteen minutes for a photoshoot with Phoebe Bridgers in a sticky bar booth deep in the belly of an old converted cargo ship, moored in the Mud Dock area of Bristol's Floating Harbour. Don't ever tell me that the music industry isn't glamorous! Soundcheck is running behind schedule but Phoebe and I get some great portraits. Just as the venue staff decide they can't hold the punters back any longer, I manage to quickly hop onto the stage and take a couple of shots of the guitar rig, while a steady crowd of slightly soggy revellers pour in through the hatches.

It's one of Phoebe's earliest UK tours following the release of her 2017 debut album, *Stranger in the Alps*, a record that set the standard for her beautiful songwriting and scathingly astute lyrical observations, all delivered in deceptively sweet tones. Phoebe began writing songs while strumming and fingerpicking on an acoustic guitar in the traditional style, but one day in the studio, a chance suggestion by a producer placed a baritone in her hands, and Phoebe never looked back.

At live shows, Phoebe often plays a black sparkle Danelectro 56 Baritone in open tunings, which gives depth to her distinctive, melancholic indie-pop sound. Baritones, with their low register, are an unusual choice for a female singer and more typically heard in modern metal, but when something works, it works, and the results here are undeniable.

Phoebe's surge in popularity marks an interesting demographic shift for guitar music. Both her solo albums and her work with all-female supergroup boygenius are massively popular with teenage girls, yet sexist double standards die hard. This was demonstrated when Phoebe smashed her guitar, another Danelectro baritone, at the end of a 2021 *SNL* performance of "I Know the End" from her hit album *Punisher*. In a dramatic finale to her performance, Phoebe hammered her jet-black guitar against the on-stage monitors, sparking a tidal wave of debate – particularly online – with artists from across the musical spectrum weighing in with their opinions.

Guitar-smashing has been a popular act of defiance for so long that it has become somewhat of a rock 'n' roll trope for which many male artists are lauded – the fragments of instruments trashed by the likes of Pete Townshend, Jimi Hendrix and Kurt Cobain have been displayed at museums and sold for huge sums at auction. Some guitarists even have cheaper guitars specifically designed to be smashed, so expected is it as a part of their stage act. Yet when a woman dares to express herself with that same level of catharsis, it sparks judgement and debate, and a whole lot of negativity from male commentators.

Clearly, we still have a long way to go and women in music still have to work twice as hard for half the recognition, but with unapologetic female role models such as Phoebe Bridgers at the forefront of modern pop music, hopefully future generations of female guitarists will find that some of the barriers have been broken down.

ANELECTRO

For Chris, my guitar hero.

First published in 2024 by Welbeck
An imprint of HEADLINE PUBLISHING GROUP

1

Cataloguing in Publication Data is available from the British Library

UK ISBN: 9781802798395
USA ISBN: 9781035421787

Printed and bound in China

Headline's policy is to use papers that are natural, renewable and recyclable products and made from wood grown in well-managed forests and other controlled sources. The logging and manufacturing processes are expected to conform to the environmental regulations of the country of origin.

HEADLINE PUBLISHING GROUP
An Hachette UK Company
Carmelite House
50 Victoria Embankment
London EC4Y ODZ

www.headline.co.uk
www.hachette.co.uk

Kurt Cobain's "Smells Like Teen Spirit" 1969 Fender Competition Mustang featured courtesy of James S. Irsay and The Jim Irsay Collection, LLC.

Jimi Hendrix's 1968 Fender Stratocaster, Woody Guthrie's 1936 Martin 000-18 and Howlin' Wolf's 1965 Epiphone Casino featured courtesy of the Museum of Pop Culture, Seattle, WA.